Billy Wilder on Assignment

Billy Wilder on Assignment

DISPATCHES FROM WEIMAR BERLIN

AND INTERWAR VIENNA

Edited by Noah Isenberg

Translated by Shelley Frisch

Princeton University Press
Princeton and Oxford

Requests for permission to reproduce material from this work
should be sent to permissions@press.princeton.edu

Published by Princeton University Press
41 William Street, Princeton, New Jersey 08540
6 Oxford Street, Woodstock, Oxfordshire OX20 1TR

press.princeton.edu

Grateful acknowledgment is made for permission to reprint the
following previously published material:
Figures 8, 9, 12, and 13, from Deutsche Kinemathek.
Figure 14, from Österreichische Nationalbibliothek.
Figures 1, 2, 4, 5, 6, 7, 10, and 11, from Filmarchiv Austria.

Library of Congress Cataloging-in-Publication Data

Names: Wilder, Billy, 1906–2002, author. | Isenberg, Noah William, editor. |
Frisch, Shelley Laura, translator.
Title: Billy Wilder on assignment : dispatches from Weimar Berlin and
interwar Vienna / edited by Noah Isenberg ; translated by Shelley Frisch.
Other titles: Articles. Selections. English.
Description: Princeton : Princeton University Press, [2021] | Includes index. |
In English, translated from the original German.
Identifiers: LCCN 2020021170 (print) | LCCN 2020021171 (ebook) |
ISBN 9780691194943 (hardback) | ISBN 9780691214559 (ebook)
Subjects: LCSH: Journalism—Germany—Berlin—History—20th century. |
Journalism—Austria—Vienna—History—20th century. | Theater—Reviews. |
Motion pictures—Reviews. | Berlin (Germany)—Social life and customs. |
Vienna (Austria)—Social life and customs. | Berlin (Germany)—
History—1918–1945. | Vienna (Austria)—History—1918-
Classification: LCC PN4725 .W54 2021 (print) | LCC PN4725 (ebook) |
DDC 073–dc23
LC record available at https://lccn.loc.gov/2020021170
LC ebook record available at https://lccn.loc.gov/2020021171

British Library Cataloging-in-Publication Data is available

Jacket art: (1) Portrait: Filmarchiv Austria; (2) background image:
Potsdamer Platz, Berlin, ca. 1930, INTERFOTO / Alamy

This book has been composed in Adobe Garamond Pro

Printed on acid-free paper. ∞

Printed in the United States of America

10 9 8 7 6 5 4 3 2 1

Contents

Editor's Introduction: A Roving Reporter, a Tale of
  Two Cities, and the Making of Billy Wilder   1

**I. Extra! Extra! Reportage, Opinion Pieces,
and Features from Real Life**   19

"Waiter, A Dancer, Please!"   23

Promenaden-Café   42

That's Some Cold Weather—in Venice!   43

This Is Where Christopher Columbus Came into
  the Old World   47

The Art of Little Ruses   50

Naphthalene   52

Anything but Objectivity!   54

When It's Eighty-four Degrees   56

Day of Destiny   58

Wanted: Perfect Optimist   60

Renovation: An Ode to the Coffeehouse   63

Why Don't Matches Smell That Way Anymore?   65

The Rose of Jericho   68

Little Economics Lesson   69

Film Terror: On the Threat of Being Photographed   72

Berlin Rendezvous   74

Night Ride over Berlin   76

The Business of Thirst: What People Are
  Drinking Nowadays   78

Here We Are at Film Studio 1929   80

How We Shot Our Studio Film   83

Getting Books to Readers   87

How I Pumped Zaharoff for Money   90

**II. Portraits of Extraordinary and
Ordinary People**   95

Asta Nielsen's Theatrical Mission   97

My "Prince of Wales"   100

Lubitsch Discovers: A Casting by America's
  Great Director   103

The Tiller Girls Are Here!   105

The Tiller Girls' Boarding School at the Prater   107

Girardi's Son Plays Jazz at the Mary Bar   110

Paul Whiteman, His Mustache, the Cobenzl,
  and the Taverns   111

Whiteman Triumphs in Berlin   115

I Interview Mr. Vanderbilt   118

The Prince of Wales Goes on Holiday   121

Chaplin II and the Others at the Scala   124

The Lookalike Man: Tale of a Chameleon
   Named Erwin   126

A Minister on Foot   129

Interview with a Witch: Women's Newest Profession   131

Grock, the Man Who Makes the World Laugh   134

Ten Minutes with Chaliapin   137

Claude Anet in Berlin   139

At the Home of the Oldest Woman in Berlin   140

Felix Holländer   141

The Elder Statesman of Berlin Theater Critics   143

The *B. Z.* Lady and the German Crown Prince   145

Stroheim, the Man We Love to Hate   148

A Poker Artist: The Magic of Fritz Herrmann   152

"Hello, Mr. Menjou?"   157

Klabund Died a Year Ago   161

III. Film and Theater Reviews   165

Broken Barriers (1924)   167

Marital Conflicts (1927)   168

Eichberg Shoots a Film   169

The Beggar from Cologne Cathedral (1927)   170

Ole and Axel at the North Sea Shore (1927)   171

Radio Magic (1927)   172

Frost in the Studio: A Bath at Twenty Degrees
   Fahrenheit   173

Ole and Axel at Beba Palace   173

His Wife's Lover (1928)   174

From the Studios   175

Greed (1924)   176

A Blonde for a Night (1928)   176

The Valley of the Giants (1927)   177

The Last Night (1928)   177

In the Name of the Law (1922)   178

Sounds Are Recorded: The Studio Shots   179

The Threepenny Opera, for the Fiftieth Time   181

Springtime in Palestine (1928)   181

First Silhouette Sound Film   182

What a Woman Dreams in Spring (1929)   183

"Youth Stage"?   184

Stroll through the Studios—They're Shooting
    Silent Films   185

The Missing Will (1929)   188

The Winged Horseman (1929)   188

Men without Work (1929)   189

The Merry Musicians (1930)   190

Susie Cleans Up (1930)   190

Translator's Note   193

Index   197

Billy Wilder on Assignment

Editor's Introduction

Long before the award-winning Hollywood screenwriter and director Billy Wilder spelled his first name with a *y*, in faithful adherence to the ways of his adopted homeland, he was known—and widely published—in Berlin and Vienna as Billie Wilder. At birth, on June 22, 1906, in a small Galician town called Sucha, less than twenty miles northwest of Kraków, he was given the name Samuel in memory of his maternal grandfather. His mother, Eugenia, however, preferred the name Billie. She had already taken to calling her first son, Wilhelm, two years Billie's senior, Willie. As a young girl, Eugenia had crossed the Atlantic and lived in New York City for several years with a jeweler uncle in his Madison Avenue apartment. At some point during that formative stay, she caught a performance of Buffalo Bill's Wild West touring show, and her affection for the exotic name stuck, even without the *y*, as did her intense, infectious love for all things American. "Billie was her American boy," insists Ed Sikov in *On Sunset Boulevard*, his definitive biography of the internationally acclaimed writer-director.

Wilder spent the first years of his life in Kraków, where his father, the Galician-born Max (*né* Hersch Mendel), had started his career in the restaurant world as a waiter and then, after Billie's birth, as the manager of a small chain of railway cafés along the Vienna-to-Lemberg line. When this gambit lost steam, Max opened a hotel and restaurant known as Hotel City in the heart of Kraków, not far from the Wawel Castle. A hyperactive child, known for flitting about with bursts of speed and energy, Billie was prone to troublemaking: he developed an early habit of swiping tips left on the tables at his father's hotel restaurant and of snookering unsuspecting guests at the pool table. After all, he was the rightful bearer of a last name that conjures up, in both German and English, a devilish assortment of idiomatic expressions suggestive of a feral beast, a wild man, even a lunatic. "Long before Billy Wilder was Billy Wilder," his second wife, Audrey, once remarked, "he behaved like Billy Wilder."

The Wilder family soon moved to Vienna, where assimilated Jews of their ilk could better pursue their dreams of upward mobility. They lived in an apartment in the city's First District, the hub of culture and commerce, just across the Danube from the Leopoldstadt, the neighborhood known for its unusually high concentration of recently arrived Jews from Galicia and other regions of the Austro-Hungarian Empire. When the monarchy collapsed, after the First World War, the Wilders were considered to be subjects of Poland and, despite repeated efforts, were unable to attain Austrian citizenship. Billie attended secondary school in the city's Eighth District, in the so-called Josefstadt, but his focus was often elsewhere. Across the street from his school was a tawdry "hotel by the hour" called the Stadion; he liked to watch for hours on end as patrons went in and out, trying to imagine the kinds of human transactions taking place inside. He also spent long hours in the dark catching matinees at the Urania, the Rotenturm Kino, and other cherished Viennese movie houses. Any chance to take in a picture show, to watch a boxing match, or land a seat in a card game was a welcome chance for young Billie.

Although Wilder *père* had other plans for his son—a respectable, stable career in the law, an exalted path for good Jewish boys of interwar Vienna—Billie was drawn, almost habitually, to the seductive world of urban and popular culture and to the stories generated and told from within it. "I just fought with my father to become a lawyer," he recounted for filmmaker Cameron Crowe in *Conversations with Wilder*: "That I didn't want to do, and I saved myself, by having become a newspaperman, a reporter, very badly paid." As he explains a bit further in the same interview, "I started out with crossword puzzles, and I signed them." (Toward the end of his life, after having racked up six Academy Awards, Wilder told his German biographer that it wasn't so much the awards he was most proud of, but rather that his name had appeared twice in the *New York Times* crossword puzzle: "once 17 across and once 21 down.")

In the weeks leading up to Christmas 1924, at a mere eighteen years of age and fresh out of *gymnasium* (high school) with diploma in hand, Billie wrote to the editorial staff at *Die Bühne*, one of the two local tabloids that were part of the media empire belonging to a shifty Hungarian émigré named Imré Békessy, to ask how he might go about becoming a journalist, maybe even a foreign correspondent. Somewhat naïvely, he thought this could be his ticket to America. He received an answer, not the one he was hoping for, explaining that without complete command of English he wouldn't stand a chance.

Never one to give up, Billie paid a visit to the office one day early in the new year and, exploiting his outsize gift of gab, managed to talk his way in. In subsequent interviews, he liked to tell of how he landed his first job at *Die Bühne* by walking in on the paper's chief theater critic, a certain Herr Doktor Liebstöckl, having sex with his secretary one Saturday afternoon. "You're lucky I was working overtime today," he purportedly

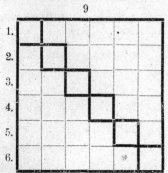

Buchstabenrätsel
9

a, a, a, a, a, c, d, d, e, e, e, e, h, j, l, l, l,
m, n, n, n, n, n, n, o, o, o, r, r, r, r, s, s,
u, w, w.

1. Wiener Kabarettkünstlerin.
2. Berühmter Sänger. †
3. Ungarischer Schriftsteller.
4. Berliner Schriftsteller.
5. Wiener Komponist. †
6. Wiener Schauspieler.

Aus diesen 36 Buchstaben sind 6 Wörter von obiger Bedeutung zu bilden. Die Diagonalbuchstaben ergeben, von oben nach unten gelesen, den Namen eines hervorragenden verstorbenen Wiener Schauspielers.

Billie Wilder

FIGURE 1. Crossword puzzle by Billie Wilder, *Die Bühne*, 1925.

told Billie. (It's hard not to think of the cast of characters that emerge from the pages of his later screenplays—the sex-starved men in his American directorial debut *The Major and the Minor* [1942] or in *Love in the Afternoon* [1957] or *The Apartment* [1960]—who bear a strong family resemblance to Herr Liebstöckl.) Soon he was schmoozing with journalists, poets, actors, the theater people who trained with Max Reinhardt, and the coffeehouse wits who gathered at Vienna's Café Herrenhof.

DIE BÜHNE

FIGURE 2. Group portrait of the Max Reinhardt Circle in the countryside, *Die Bühne* (August 6, 1925). *From left to right:* Bianca Békessy, Dr. Hans Liebstöckl, Dr. Eugen Lazar, Sybille Binder, Lina Wolwode, Billie Wilder, Louis Rainer, Annie Körner, Director Ludwig Körner, Mrs. Witzmann, Editor in Chief Emmerich (Imré) Békessy, Gitta Lazar, Theodor Danegger, Camilla Gerzhofer, Max Gülstorff, Architect Karl Witzmann.

There he met writers Alfred Polgar and Joseph Roth, a young Hungarian stage actor named Laszlo Löwenstein (later known to the world as Peter Lorre), and the critic and aphorist Anton Kuh. "Billie is by profession a keeper of alibis," observed Kuh with a good bit of sarcasm. "Wherever something is going on, he has an alibi. He was born into the world with an alibi, according to which Billie wasn't even present when it occurred."

BILLIE S. WILDER
Reporter der *STUNDE*

FIGURE 3. Billie Wilder's visiting card while a reporter for *Die Stunde*.

The Viennese journalistic scene at the time was anything but dull, and Billie bore witness, alibi or no alibi, to the contemporary debates, sex, and violence that occurred in his midst. He carried with him a visiting card with his name ("Billie S. Wilder") emblazoned upon it, and underneath it the name of the other Békessy tabloid, *Die Stunde*, to which he contributed crossword puzzles, short features, movie reviews, and profiles. Around the time he was filing his freelance pieces at a rapid clip, a fiery feud was taking place between Békessy and Karl Kraus, the acid-tongued don of Viennese letters, editor and founder of *Die Fackel* (*The Torch*), who was determined to drive the Hungarian "scoundrel" out of the city and banish him once and for all from the world of journalism. To add to this volatile climate, just months after Billie began working for the tabloid, one of *Die Stunde*'s most famous writers, the Viennese novelist Hugo Bettauer, author of the best-selling novel *Die Stadt ohne Juden* (*The City Without Jews*, 1922), was gunned down by a proto-Nazi thug.

"I was brash, bursting with assertiveness, had a talent for exaggeration," Wilder told his German biographer Hellmuth Karasek, "and was convinced that in the shortest span of time I'd learn to ask shameless questions without restraint." He was right, and soon gained precious access to everyone from international movie stars like Asta Nielsen and Adolphe Menjou, the royal celebrity Prince of Wales (Edward VIII)—to whom he devoted two separate pieces—and the American heir and newspaper magnate Cornelius Vanderbilt IV. "In a single morning," he boasted in a 1963 interview with *Playboy*'s Richard Gehman, speaking of his earliest days as a journalist in Vienna, "I interviewed Sigmund Freud, his colleague Alfred Adler, the playwright and novelist Arthur Schnitzler, and the composer Richard Strauss. In *one* morning." And while there may not be any extant articles to corroborate such audacious claims, he did manage to interview the world-famous British female dance troupe the Tiller Girls, whose arrival at Vienna's Westbahnhof station in April 1926 the nineteen-year-old Billie happily chronicled for *Die Bühne*. A mere two months later he got his big break, when the American jazz orchestra leader Paul Whiteman paid a visit to Vienna. There's a wonderful photograph of Billie in a snap-brim hat, hands resting casually in his suit-jacket pockets, a cocksure grin on his face, standing just behind Whiteman, as if to ingratiate himself as deeply as possible; after publishing a successful interview and profile in *Die Stunde*, he was invited to tag along for the Berlin leg of the tour.

In his conversations with Cameron Crowe, Wilder describes visiting Whiteman at his hotel in Vienna after the interview he conducted with him. "In my broken English, I told him that I was anxious to see him perform. And Whiteman told me, 'If you're eager to hear me, to hear the big band, you can come with me to Berlin.' He paid for my trip, for a week there or something. And I accepted it. And I packed up my things, and I

FIGURE 4. Billie Wilder, second from right, with Paul Whiteman and his band, 1926.

never went back to Vienna. I wrote the piece about Whiteman for the paper in Vienna. And then I was a newspaperman for a paper in Berlin." Serving as something of a press agent and tour guide—a role he'd play once more when American filmmaker Allan Dwan would spend his honeymoon in Berlin and, among other things, would introduce Billie to the joys of the dry martini—Wilder reviewed Whiteman's German premiere at the Grosses Schauspielhaus, which took place before an audience of thousands. "The 'Rhapsody in Blue,' a composition that created quite a stir over in the States," he writes, "is an experiment in exploiting the rhythms of American folk music. When Whiteman plays it, it is a great piece of artistry. He has to do encores again and again. The normally standoffish people of Berlin are singing his praises. People stay on in the theater half an hour after the concert."

Often referred to as Chicago on the Spree, as Mark Twain once dubbed it, Berlin in the mid-1920s had a certain New

World waft to it. A cresting wave of *Amerikanismus*—a seemingly bottomless love of dancing the Charleston, of cocktail bars and race cars, and a world-renowned nightlife that glimmered amid a sea of neon advertisements—had swept across the city and pervaded its urban air. It was a perfect training ground for Billie's ultimate migration to America, and a place that afforded him a freedom that he hadn't felt in Vienna. As the film scholar Gerd Gemünden has remarked in his illuminating study of Wilder's American career, "the American-influenced metropolis of Berlin gave Wilder the chance to reinvent himself."

During his time in Berlin, Wilder had a number of mentors who helped guide his career. First among them was the Prague-born writer and critic Egon Erwin Kisch, one of the leading newspapermen of continental Europe, who was known to hold court at his table—the "Tisch von Kisch," as it was called—at the Romanisches Café on Kurfürstendamm, a favorite haunt among Weimar-era writers, artists, and entertainers. (Wilder would hatch the idea for the film *Menschen am Sonntag* [*People on Sunday*, 1930]—on café napkins, the story goes—at the Romanisches a handful of years later.) Kisch not only read drafts of Wilder's early freelance assignments in Berlin, offering line edits and friendly encouragement, but helped him procure a furnished apartment just underneath him in the Wilmersdorf section of the city. A well-traveled veteran journalist, Kisch had long fashioned himself as *Der rasende Reporter* (*The Racing Reporter*), the title he gave to the collection of journalistic writings he published in Berlin in 1925, serving as an inspiration and role model for Billie (a caricature of Wilder from the period encapsulates that very spirit).

"His reporting was built like a good movie script," Wilder later remarked of Kisch. "It was classically organized in three acts and was never boring for the reader." In an article on the German book market, published in 1930 in the literary magazine

Eine Minute später steh' ich auf dem Gang; rekapituliere alle Daten. Dann zieh' ich den Bleistift aus meiner Brusttasche und werfe ihn die zwei Stockwerke hinab, in den Keller.

Billie.

FIGURE 5. Caricature of Billie as a "racing reporter," *Die Bühne* (February 18, 1926).

Der Querschnitt, he makes special reference to Kisch's *Paradies Amerika* (*Paradise America*, 1929), perhaps a conscious nod to the nascent Americanophilia that was already blossoming inside him.

Among the best-known dispatches of the dozens that Billie published during his extended stint as a freelance reporter was his four-part series for the *Berliner Zeitung am Mittag* (*B. Z.*), later reprinted in *Die Bühne*, on his experiences working as a dancer for hire at the posh Eden Hotel. The piece bore an epigraph from yet another of his Berlin mentors, the writer Alfred Henschke, who published under the nom de plume Klabund and was married to the prominent cabaret and theater actress Carola Neher. In it, Klabund advises young writers, gesturing toward the contemporary aesthetic trend of *Neue Sachlichkeit* (New Objectivity), to write about events as they really occurred: "The only thing that still interests us today about literature is the raw materials it's made of: life, actuality, reality." Since it's Wilder, of course, the truth is mixed with a healthy dose of droll, martini-dry humor and a touch of unavoidable poetic license as he recounts the gritty details of his trade: the wealthy ladies of leisure who seek his services, the jealous husbands who glare at him, and the grueling hours of labor on the dance floor. "I wasn't the best dancer," he later said of this period, "but I had the best dialogue."

Early on in the same piece, he includes a review of his performance attributed to the hotel management that in many ways serves as an apt summation of his whole career: "Herr Wilder knew how to adapt to the fussiest audiences in every way in his capacity as a dancer. He achieved success in his position and always adhered to the interests of the establishment." He put the skills he acquired on the dance floor to continued use on the page and on the screen, always pleasing his audience and ensuring his path to success. "I say to myself: I'm a fool," he writes in a moment of intense self-awareness. "Sleepless nights, misgivings, doubts? The revolving door has thrust me into despair, that's for sure. Outside it is winter, friends from the Romanisches Café, all with colds, are debating sympathy and poverty, and, just like me, yesterday, have no idea where to spend the night. I, however, am a dancer. The big wide world will wrap its arms around me."

An ideal match for Billie arrived when, in 1928, the Ullstein publishing house, publisher of the *Berliner Zeitung am Mittag,* introduced a new afternoon *Boulevard-Zeitung,* an illustrated paper aimed at a young readership and bearing a title that would speak directly to them and to Wilder: *Tempo.* "It was a tabloid," remarked historian Peter Gay in his early study of the "German-Jewish Spirit" of the city, "racy in tone, visual in appeal, designed to please the Berliner who ran as he read." The Berliners, however, quickly adopted another name for it: they called it *jüdische Hast,* or "Jewish haste." Billie, an inveterate pacer and man on the move, was a good fit for *Tempo* and vice versa (it was in its pages that he introduced Berliners to the short-lived independent production company Filmstudio 1929 and the young cineastes, including Wilder himself, behind its creation).

In 1928, after serving as an uncredited ghostwriter on a number of screenplays, Billie earned a solo writing credit for a picture that had more than a slight autobiographical bearing on its author. It was called *Der Teufelsreporter* (*Hell of a Reporter*), though it also bore the subtitle *Im Nebel der Großstadt* (*In the Fog of the Metropolis*), and was directed by Ernst Laemmle, nephew of Universal boss Carl Laemmle. Set in contemporary Berlin, it tells the story of the titular character, a frenetic newspaperman played by American actor Eddie Polo, a former circus star, who works at a city tabloid—called *Rapid*, in explicit homage—and whose chief attributes are immediately traceable to Wilder himself. Unsurprisingly, perhaps, young Billie even has a brief appearance in the film, dressed just like the other reporters in his midst. "He performs this cameo," write German film scholars Rolf Aurich and Wolfgang Jacobsen, "as if to prove who the true *Teufelsreporter* is." In addition to asserting a deeper connection to the city and to American-style tabloid journalism, *Der Teufelsreporter* lays a foundation for other hard-boiled newspapermen in Wilder's Hollywood repertoire, from Chuck Tatum (Kirk Douglas) in *Ace in the Hole* (1951) to Walter Burns (Walter Matthau) in *The Front Page* (1974).

Further affinities between Wilder's Weimar-era writings and his later film work abound. For example, in "Berlin Rendezvous," an article he published in the *Berliner Börsen Courier* in early 1927, he writes about the favored meeting spots within the city, including the oversized clock, called the *Normaluhr*, at the Berlin Zoo railway station. Two years later, when writing his script for *Menschen am Sonntag* (*People on Sunday*, 1930), he located the pivotal rendezvous between two of his amateur protagonists,

FIGURE 6. Lobby card for the film *Der Teufelsreporter* (*Hell of a Reporter*, 1928).

Wolfgang von Waltershausen and Christl Ehlers, at precisely the same spot. For the same script, he crafted the character of Wolfgang, a traveling wine salesman and playboy, as a seeming wish-fulfillment fantasy of his own exploits as a dancer for hire. Likewise, in his early account of the Tiller Girls arriving by

FIGURE 7. Billie Wilder appears in a cameo, second from left, in *Der Teufelsreporter.*

train in Vienna, there's more than a mere germ of Sweet Sue and Her Society Syncopators, the all-girl band in *Some Like It Hot* (1959); there's even a Miss Harley ("the shepherdess of these little sheep"), anticipating the character of Sweet Sue herself. In a short comic piece on casting, Billie pays tribute to director Ernst Lubitsch, a future mentor in Hollywood (many years later, Wilder's office in Beverly Hills featured a mounted plaque designed by Saul Bass with the words "How Would Lubitsch Do It?" emblazoned on it). Finally, in his 1929 profile of Erich von Stroheim, in *Der Querschnitt*, among the many things young Billie highlights is Gloria Swanson's performance in Stroheim's late silent, *Queen Kelly* (1929). It was the first flicker of the inspired idea to cast Swanson and Stroheim as a pair of

FIGURE 8. Berlin as it appears in *Menschen am Sonntag* (*People on Sunday*, 1929).

crusty, vaguely twisted emissaries from the lost world of silent cinema in *Sunset Boulevard* (1950).

•

By the time Wilder boarded a British ocean liner, the S.S. *Aquitania*, bound for America in January 1934, he'd managed to acquire a few more screen credits and a little more experience in show business, but very little of the English language (he purportedly packed secondhand copies of Ernest Hemingway's *A Farewell to Arms*, Sinclair Lewis's *Babbit*, and Thomas Wolfe's *Look Homeward, Angel* in his suitcase). He had gone from a salaried screenwriter at UFA in Berlin to an unemployed refugee in Paris to an American transplant with twenty dollars and a

FIGURE 9. Wolfgang von Waltershausen with Christl Ehlers and Brigitte Borchert in *Menschen am Sonntag*.

FIGURE 10. Wilder, at center, with Peter Lorre and other central European refugees in Hollywood.

hundred English words in his possession. "He paced his way across the Atlantic," remarks Sikov. And soon he'd pace his way onto the lot of MGM, Paramount, and other major film studios, joining an illustrious group of central European refugees who would forever change the face of Hollywood.

Wilder's acclaimed work in Hollywood, as a screenwriter and director, is in many ways an outgrowth of his stint as a reporter in interwar Vienna and Weimar Berlin. His was a raconteur's cinema, long on smart, snappy dialogue, short on visual acrobatics. "For Wilder the former journalist, words have a special, almost material quality," comments German critic Claudius Seidl. "Words are what give his films their buoyancy, elegance, and their characteristic shape, since words can fly faster, glide more elegantly, can spin more than any camera." Wilder's deep-seated attachment to the principal tools of his trade as a writer is recognizable throughout his filmic career. He even provided an apt coda, uttered by none other than fading silent screen star Norma Desmond (Gloria Swanson) in *Sunset Boulevard*, when she learns that Joe Gillis (William Holden) is a writer: "words, words, more words!"

A Note on the Text

To give the reader the most representative selection of Billy Wilder's writings from the period, we have drawn on two separate German-language anthologies: *Der Prinz von Wales geht auf Urlaub: Berliner Reportagen, Feuilletons und Kritiken der zwanziger Jahre* (Berlin: Fannei und Waltz, 1996), a collection of Wilder's Berlin-based journalism from the second half of the 1920s edited by Klaus Siebenhaar; and *"Billie": Billy Wilders Wiener journalistische Arbeiten* (Vienna: Filmarchiv Austria, 2006), a companion volume of Wilder's Viennese publications from the mid-1920s, co-edited by Rolf Aurich, Wolfgang Jacobsen, and Günter Krenn.

We have organized the pieces into three separate sections, defined by formal and thematic categories. In some instances, we opted not to include pieces that seemed either too esoteric, too anachronistic, or simply inaccessible to an Anglo-American audience. We believe the selection we have chosen gives the greatest sense of Wilder's unique voice, his budding skills as a writer, his wit and intelligence, and his range.

Finally, we'd like to thank the Billy and Audrey L. Wilder Foundation for their very kind support of our effort to bring Wilder's early writings to an English-language audience.

I

Extra! Extra!

REPORTAGE, OPINION PIECES, AND FEATURES FROM REAL LIFE

Between September 1925 and November 1930, Wilder published dozens of freelance pieces. He began in the pages of Vienna's *Die Bühne* and *Die Stunde* (where he started out as a reporter in his teens), to which he continued to contribute intermittently after relocating to Berlin in the summer of 1926, just after his twentieth birthday. There he became a regular contributor to the *Berliner Zeitung* (or the *B. Z.*, as it was more commonly known) and the *Berliner Börsen Courier*, where he worked as a night editor from April to December 1927. In the late 1920s, while still hanging his hat in Berlin, he wrote for *Tempo*, the Ullstein publishing concern's short-lived illustrated magazine aimed at a youthful audience, and for *Der Querschnitt*, the publishing house's more highbrow literary magazine (which was something of a distant cousin to the *New Yorker*).

One of the principal genres in which young Billie trafficked was the feuilleton, or cultural essay, a potent mix of reportage and descriptive musings, which had gained considerable popularity in the newspapers—broadsheets and tabloids—of western and central Europe in the late nineteenth and early twentieth centuries. Wilder's feuilletons often took the form of jaunty, mordant, self-stylized personal essays; on occasion they read a bit more like the pointed writing we find on today's op-ed pages.

FIGURE 11. Title page of the four-part article "Herr Ober, bitte einen Tänzer!"—in which Wilder describes his days as a hotel dancer for hire—from its reprint in *Die Bühne* (June 2, 1927).

The following selection includes travel pieces (on the urban history and lore of such cities as Venice, Genoa, and Monte Carlo, and even an imagined dispatch from New York City); a pair of heartfelt tributes to the coffeehouse; a long-form essay on the book market circa 1930; and a piece devoted to the art of getting by as an impoverished freelancer. There are numerous articles specific to the contemporary scene in Berlin, among them a four-part eyewitness account of being a dancer for hire, which cast light on the darker corners of the German capital in the late 1920s while also presenting key facets of Wilder himself. In "When It's Eighty-Four Degrees," his witty reflections on a sudden heat wave, he describes Berliners dancing the Black Bottom—an American Jazz Age craze that had crossed the Atlantic to inspire legions of dance fanatics during the Weimar years—despite the inhospitable temperatures. Billie's love of speed, and of shiny new objects, finds expression in "Night Flight over Berlin," his report on the beginnings of commercial air travel in Europe, while "Berlin Rendezvous" not only plants some of the seeds of his script for *Menschen am Sonntag* (*People on Sunday*, 1930)—which he describes here in affectionate detail and with the panache of a savvy press agent in "Here We Are at Film Studio 1929," noting a certain "reportage" as its basis—but also captures the romance of the city at an especially exciting, if equally fragile, moment.

"Waiter, A Dancer, Please!"

FROM THE LIFE OF A DANCER FOR HIRE

I. I'm Looking for a Job

First, a letter, complete with a motto:

> Dear B. W.—Write your memoirs of a dancer for hire. The only thing that still interests us today about literature is the raw materials it's made of: life, actuality, reality. The motto of "vitalism" is: Every living thing is but a metaphor—Yours, Klabund

So don't be ashamed of what you've done. Don't even offer up the excuse: "A job is a job," or "It's no disgrace to work." Come straight out with it.

I received my dismissal as a dancer for hire as requested, and my record of that is in my wallet:

Record!

Herr Billie Wilder was employed in our establishment as a Social Dancer from October 15, 1926, until today.

Herr Wilder knew how to adapt to the fussiest audiences in every way in his capacity as a dancer. He achieved success in his position and always adhered to the interests of the establishment.

Herr Wilder is parting ways with our business at his own request.

The Management of the . . . Hotel.

Berlin W.

So I have it in black and white that I was a dancer, a social dancer, in a word: a dancer for hire, for two months, and one who "knew how to adapt to the fussiest audiences in every way," at that.

That's what happened, and here's how: I was not doing well—

My trousers aren't ironed, my face is badly shaved, my collar greasy, the cuffs of my shirt folded over. My tongue tastes bitter, my legs are leaden, my stomach is so empty that it's hurting, and my nerves are shot. Behind every knock on the door the venomous face of the landlady, shrieking, with the bill in her hands. For me the street is made up of gourmet food stores, restaurants, and pastry shops, and I cut my cigarettes in half to make them last longer.

I was not doing well.

Today I'll be sleeping in the waiting room of the train station.

Sad financial reckoning in front of a cigarette store:

Eleven pfennigs, another five in my vest, that comes to sixteen. "Four for four!"

That makes it easier to move on. But where to?

*

Potsdamer Platz. Someone is shouting through the clamor of the traffic, swinging his walking stick, smashing into a baby carriage.

"Hello! Imagine meeting you here! What, you don't recognize me? No? From the Tabarin in Vienna? Yes, of course—Roberts."

I sink through the floor in shame.

"Come for a cognac; it's on me. Got an appetite? Excellent. Caaaar—available? To Kempinski!"

And in the restaurant: "Bring me two orders of fish in mayonnaise, two beef filets, English-style, medium-rare, please, two salads, a bottle of 1917 Liebfraumilch. But first, two large Hennessys."

※

That is Roberts, the dancer: his hair is black as ink and shiny as rain-slicked asphalt, his eyes evince the South, his nose and his lips those of the dead Valentino.

He eats a hot lunch and smokes imported cigarettes, coins jingle in his pockets, he pays his rent on time, and doesn't owe a single pfennig to the washerwoman; yes, the word "inhibitions" has never crossed his mind. Maybe that's how billionaires live.

Of course, he's a dancer. Yvette and Roberts. He's danced in London and in Paris, in Warsaw, in Vienna, in Nice, in Karlsbad, in Brussels and in Rome, in San Sebastian, everywhere.

While we're eating, he tells me that he's been hired for the entire winter in Berlin. A giant hotel near the Memorial Church. Every evening, Yvette and Roberts in their dances. People are so nice to him, he adds.

"And you? What are you up to?"

I lower my head so he can't see my collar. *Well—this and that.* I tell him I don't have anything at the moment, no job, for the past three weeks already, but that something will turn up soon. I even have an idea, I say, I always have ideas.

"Can I help you?"

Roberts puts his hand on my arm. I tug on my tie and look away, read the label on the wine bottle.

"You are tall enough."

What am I—?

"You have suits, a tuxedo?"

Well, sure, well, of course, they're just in hock right now.

"You have some sense of how to bow in high society, how to kiss a woman's hand."

I'm baffled.

"You dance, I know that. Now I'm asking you: don't you want to capitalize on all that?"

My face goes blank.

"Do you want to earn money?"

I'm now slack-jawed.

"Money, lots of money!"

Not a word.

"You'll become—a dancer for hire with us. You'll present yourself tomorrow."

Then he asks for the check, pulls a hundred-mark bill out of his wallet, thereby revealing another dozen of these bills, and holds it out to the waiter.

—Yes, I'll present myself tomorrow.

II. The First Day in the Hotel

In the morning Roberts sent me two hundred marks—"to outfit you, for the time being, in a manner befitting your station." I turned over seventy-five marks to my landlady, à conto, went to the pawnshop, picked up my suitcase full of clean clothing from the washerwoman across the street, spent an hour at the barbershop, lingered just as long in front of the mirror, knotted my tie, again and again, brushed and smoothed.

I'm sitting in a club chair in the hotel lobby, a soft one, and leaning far back, one leg over the other, and am up to my tenth cigarette, at twelve pfennigs a pop. This, then, is the hotel I'm to "work" in. The bellboy at the revolving door, thinking I'm a guest, has tipped his cap gracefully. Now the Persian lamb coat of a lady in narrow, crocodile-leather shoes brushes against my knees, as she walks toward the lift, smiles at the pageboy, disappears. A thin fragrance of Coty lingers in the air, and stirs up my nerves. A valet, laden with luggage, stumbles to the door, a gentleman in a raglan coat with a stiff foot enters his name into the hotel register, while the porter, his back bent over, holds out his palm to an elderly couple, and the bartender balances two Manhattans and a soda.

I say to myself: I'm a fool. Sleepless nights, misgivings, doubts? The revolving door has thrust me into despair, that's for sure. Outside it is winter, friends from the Romanisches Café, all with colds, are debating sympathy and poverty, and, just like me, yesterday, have no idea where to spend the night. I, however, am a dancer. The big wide world will wrap its arms around me.—In the ballroom slender-legged women sit at small tables sipping mocha coffee. They're putting their cups down and sizing me up, their crimson lips puckered into a honeyed, peeved smile. The gazes of jealous husbands and spiffy friends are burning on my forehead. Dark red light spills onto the dance floor, the Spaniards on the podium squeeze a *tango argentino* out of their accordions and sing in foreign accents. I'm dancing with a woman of exotic beauty. . . . White powdered arms tightly wound around my neck, the fragrance of *Narcisse Noir* emanating from her hair . . .

*

"Slept well?"

Roberts.

"Ironed your suit? Collar clean? Proper necktie? Wait!"

Then he comes back accompanied by a young man with a pallid face, his eyes red and teary. Seems to be somewhat asleep. His hair is thinning, although he is thirty at most. Worn out.

Roberts: "This is Herr Isin, the dance instructor."

Herr Isin holds out a hand to me that is as soft as butter and lacks any bones. He prattles on about something, toneless and withdrawn. Russian.

Roberts: "Isin, you will explain everything to the gentleman. I have to go into the ballroom."

Herr Isin nods, hikes up his wide trouser legs, and sits down next to me.

"So, where have you danced?"

"Nowhere."

"I see. Amateur. Got it."

He pulls an old bus ticket out of his coat pocket and a tiny stub of a pencil, giving its tip a lick.

"I have to register you with the police. You have to pay tax. And health insurance money. What's your name?"

Thus and thus.

"Birthdate?"

This and such.

"Young, very young." Ticket and pencil disappear back into Herr Isin's pocket.

"Just the essentials. You'll dance afternoons and evenings. From 4:30 to 7:00 and from 9:30 to 1:00. Afternoons dark suit, stiff collar, evenings tuxedo. You'll eat with your colleagues. Like a guest."

Like a guest—

"As for the wages: five marks a day, making 150 a month. But don't forget, there's also . . ."

Herr Isin closes his left eye.

"Dance lessons . . . or—tips—"

The dance instructor's sallow face gives me a long and mild look. "The likes of us have never gone hungry. You'll do well."

"I'll do well. My assignment?"

"Hmm. I can't actually explain that to you. Our profession is practical application, nothing but practical application."

"Our profession—"

"You can start today," Roberts told me. "Take off your coat. I'll explain everything else to you in the ballroom."

*

The cloakroom.

"This is our new dancer."

The woman behind the desk fixes her sharp gaze on me, sharp like a military doctor. Then she says, in a thick Czech accent: "Put down coat here. But if place full, drop off at front, or else too crowd and guests have not room. Understood?"

"Of course, my lady."

In the ballroom. Packed. Cigarette haze. Perfume and brilliantine. Preened ladies from twenty to fifty. Bald heads. Mamas with prepubescent daughters. Young men with garish neckties and brightly colored spats. Whole families.

The jazz band on the upper level is slouching over their instruments and bobbing to the rhythm. Aside from the banjo player, who is looking down, bored and mouth agape, at the couples as they jump, grind, chuff, and hop.

Loud and sweltering.

Herr Isin's red eyes gaze at me as though straining to say: Go!

Yes, yes, I'll go dance. Over there in the corner, the lady in the Persian lamb coat and the crocodile leather shoes. I'll go ask her to dance.

But Herr Isin taps my shoulder. "You're dancing with table 91. Right over here."

Table 91. An older lady in a bottle-green dress, with a long neck and hair the color of egg yolks; and a little lady, whose reddish snub nose is trying too hard to look uppity.

I stand in front of them, a second Buridan's ass, sweat on my brow, showing all my colors, helpless and wobbly. Then I mechanically thrust my torso forward, toward the one with the snub nose, purse my lips, and say very softly:

"May I ask for this dance?"

She smiles at me with a sour look on her face, mulling it over.

I must look quite silly, in this comical position, blushing deeply, bowing down to her.

The little one gets up, places her chubby arm around my shoulder. We dance. The blood is pounding against my temples, my legs seem to be paralyzed by a stroke. Everything blurs until someone kicks my shin and thus revives me. An endless dance. My shirt is sticking to my body. I'm gritting my teeth. We spin on. My arms now weigh a ton. I would love to leave my dance partner standing right here, get my coat from the cloakroom, and run away, far away, to those lacking pfennigs and beds—

But Herr Isin's face is smiling, yellow and distant.

I dance only with table 91. The one with the long neck has asked for my name, letting me know that she plans to come often, now that I'm a dancer here.

III. The Colleagues

At some point, Herr Isin comes up to me.

"Have you met your colleagues? No? Come with me!"

In the red ballroom, almost at the door, four young people sit at a table and eat with abandon.

"A new colleague, Herr . . ." Herr Isin rummages through his pockets for my personnel slip; my name has slipped his mind.

"Delighted, delighted, likewise, likewise."

The four: one is named Willy and is from Vienna. He spent two years at the circus, as a performer in "Icarian games." But this job has more to offer, he says. His teeth are bad, and his hair glistens from his cheap pomade. Wouldn't it be better to stay with the circus?

I didn't quite catch the name of the second one; it ended with something like—sti. Berliner. Actually a sales representative at a paper factory. That he is now dancing for the sake of the money, is, I was told (a) a sign of the rotten times, (b) a funny whim of his. In the mornings he takes around his sample cases, in the afternoons he dances. Only in the afternoons. In the evenings he has to do his bookkeeping.

The one next to me: Kurt, nice fellow, son of good people, with a tasteful, diagonally striped necktie and a weak stomach. That's why he drinks nothing but tea. Horn-rimmed glasses. Very pleasant. He, too, is on duty only for the five o'clock tea; he, too, is not really a dancer. More like a pianist, but without steady employment. And you'd have to be well dressed for that.

Finally, the fourth one: Professeur de danse Miguel Ferrer. Spaniard. Not tall, but finely chiseled facial features. Doesn't speak a word of German, only French, Flemish, Italian, Portuguese, Dutch, and, of course, Spanish. If he has something to tell the others, he raises his fingers to his eye, his ear, puts them on his nose, crosses them over his lips, twists his elbow, and points in all directions. That is his sign language, seeing as the other three speak only German, aside from the Viennese man, who doesn't quite have a command of that language either.

A waiter serves me coffee, apple cake with whipped cream, ice cream.—Like a guest.—And I'm asked if I want more whipped cream.

Then Ferrer asks, "Parlez-vous français?"

"Mais oui."

"Épatant. Je suis heureux de pouvoir causer avec vous."*

I scrape the last bits of my pie from the plate. The other four are already on the dance floor. Willy is entwined with a chubby woman, the Spaniard is lifting his legs languidly, indifferent to the beat, but his partner doesn't notice; her little eyes are fixed on the ceiling in rapture. I'm back at work, table 91.

It's unbearably hot. My collar is as soft as pudding and totally sweaty, my arms are aching. The two bands up there are playing without a break. On the dance floor, which is just over twenty feet long and fifteen wide, there are thirty couples. The paper sales representative watches my moves, and the corners of his mouth curl into a pitying grimace: *novice*. Roberts sits at a table, quite close to the dance floor, and winks at me: *courage*. And Ferrer, who was just poked in the ribs by someone's elbow, comes out with some sort of Spanish curse word.

Seven o'clock. The ballroom is already half-empty, table 91 gone. Ferrer and I are standing at the cloakroom.

Herr Isin shows up again.

"Well?"

"How's that?"

Isin taps me on the shoulder.

"You'll get it."

Then: "Be here at 9:30. The waiter will show you where you'll eat. Adieu."

Table 103

It is bitterly cold at my place. It needs to be heated starting tomorrow, at least a little. It's not the least bit pleasant to spend two hours half-naked, pedantically carrying out my dressing routine, knotting my bow tie with fingers that have turned blue from the cold.

---

* "Splendid. I am happy to be able to chat with you."

From 7:00 to 9:30 I have a "break." Only a seeming break, because I have to spend this time changing out of the suit I was dancing in for the tea and into my tuxedo; also changing my shirt, shoes, socks. No, tomorrow there will definitely need to be a little heat. People like us can afford that, can't we, Herr Isin?

Nine thirty, in the hotel ballroom. Guests are already there. The good tables reserved for theatergoers. Ladies in silver evening gowns with coiffures that smell like burnt hair. Gentlemen in dress suits, studying the prices on the wine list through their monocles. One member of the tango band is playing a violin solo, "Butterfly." The plump woman at the corner table places her hand on her eyelids in a sentimental gesture.

❋

I sit down in some corner. Three waiters around me. One slides the complete menu under my nose, a second one the wine list, the third puts a flower vase on the table.

"The gentleman is awaiting someone, please?"

"Oh, no, I'm the new dancer."

The one with the fat cheeks and a pale goulash stain on the front of his shirt squints over at his colleague with a grin.

"Dancer? That is not here. Not yet."

To the bellboy at the door, "Take the dancer to his dining room."

My dining room can be reached by way of a wooden staircase and is set up on a balcony that is barred to the guests: two bare tables and a couple of chairs. The table on the right only for the maître d', the one on the left for the others, namely, waiters, bellboys, lift operators, porters, door openers, coffee girls, and so forth, and also for the dancers.

Ferrer, the Spaniard, and Willy, the man from Vienna, are already there. And someone else, the chauffeur for our boss, the "hotel co-owner."

Set menu for the staff: consommé—larded filet of beef with baby vegetables and Madeira sauce—parfait—a bottle of beer—countless rolls.

Well, that's wonderful. Willy always gives the little guy who serves us three cents, and he eats two portions of ice cream. "Because you have to, the Charleston makes you damned skinny, word of honor."

Herr Isin comes up, just for the inspection, because the managers eat downstairs in the main hall. A splendid tuxedo, double-breasted, wide lapels, milky white shirt, gold buttons. Shaved, coiffed, perfumed.

"Enjoyed your meal? Off to work, gentlemen." Downstairs everything is already in full swing. Good people.

Champagne.

"Go over there, to table 103. You see, a lady, a gentleman, and two young girls. Try to pounce."

"Pounce" means—Willy told me—engage the ladies, ask them to dance. I blow my nose and go over when the first fox-trot starts. With the gentleman's permission—

Oh, Papa at table 103 has absolutely nothing against my dancing with his daughters. I alternate between them. Both still have thin arms and bashful mouths. The older one, maybe seventeen and a half, nestles up against me gently. She tells me that she greatly enjoyed dancing in Neuchâtel, in Switzerland, where she was in boarding school. And she wondered if I wanted to come back for the tango. Yes. But during the tango, she no longer said a single word. No doubt Mama had strictly forbidden conversation with the dancer for hire.

Eleven thirty. Yvette and Roberts dance—Boston, Charleston, paso doble. During the main attraction, Herr Isin stands next to me.

"In the evening you dance only with tables that I instruct you to go to. Or with ladies who send for you. Be very careful."

Willy tells me he has an old customer, a Frau Doktor. Ferrer daydreams listlessly in the corner of the bar until Herr Isin directs him to three ladies who have expressed the wish to move around a bit.

It is much less comfortable than in the afternoon. The stiff shirt is torture. But the daughters at table 103 don't know the meaning of fatigue.

After midnight, the family at table 103 is preparing to leave. Papa pays, Mama pulls her sable up over her bare shoulder, and the daughters powder their cheeks, hot from dancing. The family at table 103 is moving toward the exit. As chance would have it, I am standing right next to it. The youngsters nod, Mama looks past me, but Papa goes straight up to me, holds out his hand to me, "Goodbye." I feel something in my palm, paper. They are already at the cloakroom. I put my hand into my pants pocket and run, red as a freshly boiled crab, right to the men's room, lock myself in, then slide the thing out of my pocket with two fingers.

A five-mark bill.

*

At one o'clock I'm allowed to go home.

Dead tired. I want to hang up my tuxedo in the closet, but my eyes fall shut. During this night I dream:

A man comes into my room, very close to my bed. He is slim and tall and gray, his threadbare overcoat going down to the floor. In his right hand he holds a bunch of files, in his left a tall top hat. His small, colorless mouse eyes are trained on me. Now the man places the top hat onto the night table and pulls a sheet of yellowed paper out of his bundle of documents. His thin blue lips part, and slowly and softly utter these words, "I'm garnishing you!"

"Me?" I shout. But the Tall One continues, "You owe your landlady the rent for these months: May, June, July, August,

September, October." I leap out of bed, "No, that's a lie. Paid, all paid. The receipt's in the drawer."

The Tall One doesn't make a move, his mouse eyes remain inert, only his blue lips part. "You're a dancer. I'm garnishing your knees." I raise my fists at him and holler, "No!" Suddenly I feel the blood freeze in my veins, I'm seized with horror, and my throat tightens: the Tall One doesn't hear, because he has no ears, just rosy skin, no ears.

In front of me it is the dead of night; I grow dizzy and faint back onto the bed. But the man comes at me, extends a frosty red hand to my legs, pulls the knees out of them, and gently places them into the top hat. Then he takes the hat from the night table, shoves the files under his arm, and heads to the door. I want to follow him, but I fall.

"My job, my joooob!" I babble. The Tall One stands in the doorway, turns his head, and grins. Loathsome.—I see myself again, in the ballroom. The Tall One is sitting at every table. I dance with him, in raving rhythm, Herr Isin's red eyes play ring-around-the-rosy around us, my legs buckle in a hundred places, Roberts slaps me, someone is throwing around five-mark bills, a woman cries out, and I sink, fall deep down . . .

IV. The Daily Deal

My day goes well.

I sleep well into the afternoon, until about three o'clock. Right after I was hired, I bought an alarm clock; it works flawlessly. My dressing routine now takes a good hour, and it is so grotesquely complex that I am beginning to feel ashamed of myself in front of the landlady. A whole series of new acquisitions are now in the room, beautification implements and primping potions of the kind you would expect only on ladies' vanity tables: perfume bottles, French soaps, complexion creams, white eau de cologne, violet eau de cologne, skin lotion in all colors, powder in all shades, lavender water, pomades, eyebrow brushes, fingernail polish, hair gel, this and that.

A massage is part of my bathing routine. My legs float in the soapy water, and I notice that this new job is good for their muscles. My dutiful legs, my breadwinners.

Then four minutes shaving, four minutes hairstyling, ten minutes getting my clothing ready, ten minutes necktie, eight minutes suit, five minutes final look into the mirror.

By quarter after four I have to leave the house, because the people at the hotel are punctilious about punctuality. Four thirty is the time to make my appearance.

I basically already feel at home. I actually say little to my colleagues, I'm merely there, like someone at the office. Just: *Good day, adieu, earned something? Who was the snazzy lady, you know, the one with the two gentlemen in the car? Do you have an extra cigarette? Lousy weather today*—and so forth.

*

I actually have the first stage of my training behind me. Herr Isin no longer points out the ladies I am to dance with; I choose them myself.

"Bear in mind that you are not here for your own enjoyment. You are here to dance. Including with ladies who don't appeal to you. In fact, the less they appeal to you, the more honestly and conscientiously you are doing your job. The dancer's First Commandment is: there can be no wallflowers. He needs to pluck them, because that is what he is getting paid for. Bear that in mind."

I make my living honestly, honestly and with difficulty, because I dance honestly and conscientiously. No wishes, no desires, no thoughts, no opinions, no heart, no brain. All that matters here are my legs, which belong to this treadmill and on which they have to stomp, in rhythm, tirelessly, endlessly one-two, one-two, one-two.

I dance with young and old; with the very short and those who are two heads taller than I; with the pretty and the less attractive; with the very slender and those who drink teas designed to slim them down; with ladies who send the waiter to get me and savor the tango with eyes closed in rapture; with wives, with fashion plates sporting black-rimmed monocles, and whose escorts, themselves utterly unable to dance, hire me; with painfully inept out-of-towners who think an excursion to Berlin would be pointless without five o'clock tea; with splendid women from abroad who divide their stay in Berlin between hotel rooms, halls, and ballrooms; with ladies who are there every day and no one knows where they're from and where they're going; with a thousand kinds.

❦

This is no easy way to earn your daily bread, nor is it the kind that sentimental, softhearted types can stomach. But others can live from it. I did not earn badly this first week, but starting out is typically always difficult; let's hope it goes on this way.

I won't go hungry. My average daily earning is twenty marks, plus my wages. Later it will surely get better, only practice will get me there. Willy and the Spaniard earn twice as much, but they have experience, they are better psychologists, they know their way around.

❦

The treadmill in the hotel keeps running, and with it the whole hullabaloo to which I now belong, full-fledged, like the others: the Spaniard, Willy, the paper sales representative, and Kurt.

In my notebook the reservations for dance lessons are increasing. Yesterday I was employed from ten to twelve—a family in Grunewald—and from two to four—two ladies who live in the hotel. The instructional hours alone make me forty marks. But the bad part is that I can no longer get a good night's sleep.

These past ten days I earned roughly four hundred marks. Three-quarters of this sum got eaten up by the purchase of a portable gramophone, which I now need for the classes, as well as fifteen records. Whiteman, Hylton, the Revelers, Jack Smith. On top of that, the down payment at a top-notch tailor, on Kurfürstendamm, for a suit, dark blue, finely patterned, double-breasted, six buttons; wide trousers, the latest; three neckties; a pair of black shoes; four dress shirts.

*

Saturday is the worst day for the dancer. All the halls are full to the very last seat. On the dance floor fifty couples crowd together, stepping on one another's feet, panting and sparring. One single mass of flesh, quivering in rhythm like aspic. It is a day when the dancer for hire loses a couple of pounds of weight but is unlikely to gain a single pfennig.

I position myself at the wall in the large hall and analyze all the tables. Facing away from me are two ladies, both with Eton crop hairdos and red ears.

I dance with the two Eton crops. With one of them, this dialogue ensues:

"I actually feel sorry for you, having to work so hard."

"Oh, it's a pleasure to be able to dance with my dear Madame."

"Is it?"

"It is indeed."

"And you think I dance well?"

"Superbly."

"That I cut a fine figure?"

"A fabulous one."

The eternal feminine—yet I'm nothing but a dancer for hire.

∗

It is incredible how mean people can get.

A waiter informs me: table 87 wishes to have a dancer.

Fine, I go there. But not to table 87, because I misunderstand the number; I go to table 86. Sitting at this table are a burly young man and a bulbous-nosed lady with a tangerine-colored gown that comes down to her ankles.

I make my obligatory bow in front of the couple and recite my set phrase as I face the gentleman: May I be permitted to dance with the lady?

The man turns bright red in an instant, and his dueling scars stand out like white crisscrosses. His bellowing makes all the guests in the room jump up from their seats:

"I will permit nothing of the sort. How dare you indulge in this boorish behavior? How do you figure you can harass this lady? Youuu . . . nobody!"

I can't think of absolutely anything to say in response. Dozens of curious people are now assembled around the table. I finally stammer: I beg your pardon—but I am the house dancer, and I was sent for!

"Is that so!" the man shouts back, foaming and trembling with fury. "What are you? We know these kinds of excuses."

Herr Isin is already behind me, profusely begging forgiveness for my behavior. The customer is always right.

∗

With a lovely black woman in sumptuous ermine, underneath it an evening gown that looks like a silver suit of armor, a pink rose at her hip.

She has summoned me to the table: nine courses, plus a bottle of Veuve Clicquot sec. Hither and yon we dance. She doesn't say a word; she's probably thinking: *I've rented two legs because I want to dance right now, but their owner is an idiot.*

Just once she asks, "Do you think the Black Bottom dance is coming into fashion?"

"No," I answer. And once again there is silence for two hours. We just dance. Or we sit across from each other without speaking.

At two o'clock she says, "We're going." I am to bring her home, because she's alone.

Fine by me, I think.

A taxi is already there. We get in, she says to the driver, "Kantstrasse . . ."

I'm nervous. I look through the side window at the neon signs outside, washed by the November rain. Kantstrasse. The taxi stops. I help the lady out of the car.

The taxi drives away.

She opens the front door. Suddenly, however, she wheels around, gazes into my eyes, and asks, looking dead serious: "Do you know who Kant was?"

Who Kant was? What a sweetheart. I don't want to spoil the setup for which she paid seventy-two marks, not including the car expenses.

I answer: "Of course, my dear Madame, a Swiss national hero."

She grimaces, then lifts her hand and caresses my cheek, the way you would with a poor little inane child. Then she goes into the house and locks the door behind her.

I turn up the collar of my overcoat and walk down the street.

B. Z. [Berliner Zeitung] am Mittag, January 19, 20, 22, and 24, 1927; reprinted in *Die Bühne*, June 2, 1927

Promenaden-Café

In Stockholm and in Singapore, people know just as well as they do in Cairo and Montevideo that in Vienna you need to have seen four things: the girls, St. Stephen's Cathedral, the Cobenzl Castle, and the coffeehouses.

As every child knows, the coffeehouse is a specifically Viennese affair. And now Vienna has gotten its most beautiful café. Located at the corner of Schwarzenbergplatz and Parkring, it had its opening yesterday, and its name is Promenaden-Café. Even the most pampered visitor is impressed. The elegant red hall with the charming corner arrangements, the green and the blue salon, the dining room, the appetizing food, the waiters in finest tails, all that attests to charm and good taste. And the specialty coffee! Praise be to the cook, praise to her heartwarming approach: half a cup of whipped cream swims over that wonderfully fragrant specialty coffee, the *Weisse* (you don't know when to settle down and rejoice—each tastes better than the one before). The pastry, the newspaper, cigarettes all appear quick as lightning, materializing on the marble table as if by magic. How comfortable, how patriarchal you feel in those velvet armchairs! The window, adorned with flowers, offers a splendid view onto the Ring, with the aroma of Turkish coffee under your nose. . . . No, you have to get to know this feeling for yourself! Go there and judge. I have found my favorite café.

Die Stunde, September 17, 1925

That's Some Cold Weather—in Venice!

Venice, late February.—The airplane passenger escaping the winter over the Alps sets the heat down to the halfway mark at Udine, presses his cheek against the window, closes his eyes partway, and lets the full sun shine on his nose; he stretches out his arms and legs until his joints crack, spreads out as if under a warm quilt, and stays hushed in sweet sultriness until the Italian pilot notifies him that the sky-blue thing on the left is the Adriatic Sea, and the river down below is the Piave.

From the landing place, S. Niccolò di Lido, a motorboat brings him to Venice. He sees the Canal di S. Marco, which is as smooth as a billiards table and as clear as the eyes of the Madonna del Mascoli. He slips off his glove and sticks his finger into the water, for just a second, then pulls it out again, blue with cold. But he is delighted about the South that surrounds him, devotedly lays his traveling cap on his lap, and thinks he sees the Ponte della Paglia and the Campanile over there.

Upstairs, in his hotel room, he happily opens the window and breathes in the spring. Then he takes light flannel trousers out of his suitcase, white shoes with yellow toe caps and a violet shirt, and he deeply regrets having left his straw hat at home. He walks across the Riva degli Schiavoni, bareheaded, buoyant, and revitalized. He stumbles across scuffling young rascals, orange peels fly out of laundry-laden windows onto his head; he doesn't notice any of it. A cold wind from the Isola di S. Giorgio Maggiore makes him shiver, he puts only his right hand into his trousers pocket—his left hand points to Venice and the surrounding areas—while whistling Puccini and picturing himself on the equator. Doesn't see black clouds looming up. Doesn't hear the raindrops splashing onto the pavement of the piazza. He walks across it to the Lavena confectionery. Orders gelato and a dozen postcards. Spoons some ice cream and writes to his family. I'm in Arcadia, too. And: here there's sun and paradise. And: see Venice and die. And: I swim in the nice warm Adriatic every day.

He looks out onto the grand Corso in front of the old Procuratie and joins the people there; detects something of a change in the temperature, sneezes three times, goes back to the Albergo, gets his coat and hat and praises the travel guide, where he reads, on page 12, "When the sun goes down in the late afternoon in the winter months, there is a sudden, very noticeable cooling down, on an average of at least six to ten degrees, which is disconcerting to people from the North. The best months for a trip to Venice are April to May and September to November. But the winter is also mild because of the sea and the lagoons."

The traveler buttons up his coat as far as he can and goes to supper, through wonderfully winding little streets so narrow that a good bit of mortar sticks to his elbows, over bridges with slippery steps. He eats at a tavern near the opera: gamberetti, pea soup with parmesan. Tangerines, heavy wine from Verona, eight lire a quart, and an espresso with confectioners' sugar. He wants to go dancing and asks the waiter where: *Niente*, he says.

The next morning, the man opens the window shutters out to the side and doesn't see three yards ahead of him. London fog lies all over Venice. It is also raining, and snowing with watery flakes. The mercury is a couple of lines below zero. He turns up his coat collar and walks to the Canal Grande. At the Piazzetta there are a good twenty gondolas. No dogs anywhere. Only a *rampino* with a rusty grappling hook and a wet nose with drop after drop trickling out of it, on and on. For thirty centesimi this fellow will do a run to the Osteria where the gondoliers drink grappa, white grain.

They ride along the Canal Grande, toward the Rialto Bridge: the gondolier, who sends a wide arc of spittle hurtling toward a vaporetto, and the passenger, leafing through his travel guide with chattering teeth. He reads, "On the left, the Santa Maria della Salute church, dedicated to the rescuer from the great plague. 1030. Baroque." He glances over: nothing. He adjusts his binoculars: nothing. The fog is so thick that he could cut it with a knife. He goes on to read, "On the right, Palazzo Contarini, magnificent Early Renaissance construction (1504), with half-figures over the portals."

But he doesn't see the palazzo, nor does he see the Early Renaissance or the portals or the half-figures. Only the gondolier, who wipes his mouth on his sleeve here and there.

At the Rialto the traveler goes ashore. An elderly British woman with checkered stockings and a blue face is daubing a colorful piece of canvas; it is intended as a painting of the Rialto. A boy is stoking a charcoal fire under her feet to keep them from freezing. People become blurred in the fog, coughing and hiding away half their faces in their capes. May God have mercy.

In the Merceria the man buys a thick scarf, which he winds around his neck twice. He rides up the Campanile, 316.7 feet high. The curator says, in a hoarse voice, "Signore, Lei è fortunato, perché oggi il panorama è meraviglioso, vedrá tutte le Alpi e tutto l'Adriatico."* A whole system of binoculars is set up, but our man doesn't even see Café Aurora, let alone the Alps and the Adriatic. He spends a full three hours making the rounds of the churches, the Doge's Palace, ten museums, and Pietro Lombaro's clock tower, his feet freezing the whole way. He spends a little while watching the photographer hopping

---

* "Sir, you're in luck, because today the panorama is marvelous: you'll be able to see the whole of the Alps and the whole of the Adriatic."

from one leg to the other, blowing into his cupped hands and holding them over his ears, and looks at the man selling corn. Japanese tourists have just bought three bags of grains from him and are scattering them on the ground for the pigeons.

The traveler gives a beggar a lira. The old man points to his hat, brimless and full of holes where moths have eaten away at it, then points to the pigeons tussling over the corn and states emphatically: Yesterday a pigeon dropped something onto his hat, which essentially means that there will be a full seventeen more days of fog, rain, and cold.

Brr, the traveler thinks, and goes into Café Florian. Americans are bent over newspapers as big as bedsheets, a newlywed couple is eating whipped cream with a spoon, young Venetians with wavy hair are playing Briscola, two others are playing Italian billiards, with two large balls and one small one, pins and holes in every corner.

The man orders tea. And the railway timetable.

Then he packs at the hotel, damns the ridiculous tiled stove to hell, takes two aspirin, and dreams of doges in ermine furs skating on the frozen Canal Grande.

Die Stunde, March 3, 1927

This Is Where Christopher Columbus Came into the Old World

Genoa, in February

> NULLA DOMUS TITULO DIGNIOR
> HEIC
> PATERNIS IN AEDIBUS
> CHRISTOPHERUS COLUMBUS
> PUERITIAM
> PRIMAMQUE JUVENTAM TRANSEGIT*

This inscription is on the marble slab mounted over two windows where, about 480 years ago, Christopher Columbus's diapers were hung out to dry.

I don't know whether Christopher Columbus had brothers and sisters, or whether he was an only child. No matter: the Columbus family seems to have lived in cramped quarters; this house, with windows and a marble slab—a hundred steps from the Piazza di Ferrari Ponticello—is barely thirteen feet wide, twenty-three feet long, and sixteen feet high: stone, dark gray, flat roof, and cracked walls.

The houses to the left and right have all been torn down, thus freeing up the historic stone structure in which the man who discovered America was born, and forming the corner of a little garden surrounded by a high iron lattice in which wild grass is strewn with twisted tin cans and broken bottles, a few rotted trees, and an extremely odd edifice: a poorly restored ancient Roman portico, the parts of which were dug out of the ground

---

* "There is no house more worthy of consideration than this, in which Christopher Columbus spent his childhood and first youth inside his father's walls."

eighteen years earlier during work on the Banca d'Italia. It appears to have been there since the birth of Christ and served young Columbus and his friends as a fort when they played cops and robbers.

The aforementioned marble slab and the two windows are the only adornments on the little house apart from two heavy iron doors, just recently painted dark green, and a wreath hanging under the flat roof, which is already so withered that only an expert can establish the genus and species of the flowers. The three other façades are bare.

A curiosity-seeker finds the two iron doors locked. It is still quite early in the day, with rain on and off, and a strong wind tears at the few dusty leaves that climb up the little house. A girl in clogs is walking across the street with a milk jug.

"Always closed?"

"*Si, signore.*"

"Who has the key?"

"Why, Sir?"

"Because Columbus was born here."

"And who's Columbus?"

The girl doesn't wait for the answer but keeps on walking, swinging the milk jug, and disappears into a side alley.

A Genovese taxi driver who seems to drive foreigners every once in a while is better informed: "Columbus's house is open during the summer. Two rooms with Columbus's antique furniture."

In the house across the street, which doesn't seem much newer, there is an inn, with Pierrot costumes upstairs, one yellow, one black, the display of a company that rents out masks; a veterinarian has his practice next door, and a music school promises anyone a brand-new mandolin for free if they pay a monthly fee of twenty-five lire for half a year of lessons in advance.

Twenty buildings lean against one another, crooked and crumbling, derelict and deserted, full of holes, atria, and spiral staircases, and blind alleys all leading up to the Porta di St. Andrea, which was built around 1000. Relics of city walls adhere to it. Christopher Columbus is sure to have stood under it to play *biglie*, the game with colorful balls that boys played back in Babylon and is still played in Metropolis.

*

Over tea in Hotel Miramare a stocky, chubby-cheeked American man offers me Camel cigarettes. We fall into conversation, and after half an hour the man tells me:

"A stroke of luck brought me from San Remo to Genoa, a stroke of luck, I tell you. One should not reveal one's business plans, but hmm, hmm . . . I trust you. Listen, I have discovered the house where Columbus was born here. And this discovery can bring in millions of dollars, hahaha. Do you know what I want to do? Form a consortium in America that buys up this house, haha, and takes it to New York by ship, that's how it comes and goes, haha, then open it up to the public over there for a half-dollar entrance fee. A Columbus museum, understand? We will also go to the town hall and buy the three letters Columbus wrote that are housed in the *municipale*. And from a man in Philadelphia we'll get the anchor of the sailor whose ship was the first to reach the New World. Too bad, a crying shame that the egg Columbus got to stand on its tip has long since rotted."

Berliner Börsen Courier, April 3, 1927

The Art of Little Ruses

I don't want to come right out and insist that, starting this very day, schools teach the art of lying, by which I mean using postures and facial expressions, gestures and inflections of the voice to convey the opposite of truth with sweeping powers of persuasion and achieve smashing success. I don't mean to demand it explicitly in the framework of pushing the latest educational reform, for I, too, am ensnared in a curiously outdated set of ideas, and I appreciate and honor the so-called truth. But I can easily imagine that in two or three decades lies will be regarded as an indispensable and hence utterly unobjectionable implement in our daily lives, and their correct and appropriate use could be learned systematically by employing the scientific method.

The lie as mandatory school subject, accessible to everyone and anyone, a matter entailing assiduous effort and tireless aspiration, would no longer be the privilege of the few who have a natural predisposition in this arena: that, I think, would be the consummate moral and social justification of this hitherto maligned resource on a strictly democratic basis.

This would seem to provide a path for the art of modern education, which, for some mysterious reason, has always been overlooked. Hasn't it ever occurred to you what an irresponsible waste of life, what a scholastic peculiarity it is, that in light of today's challenges, the schools—even the most progressive ones—still fail to include a Practical Life Skills subject in the curriculum? That everyone who in their earliest childhood has already mastered the square root of two, Mariotte and Gay-Lussac's law, and the years of Saint Gregory the Great's papacy has to employ his own mental powers, in his fortieth year of life, to figure out what tools, dialectical methods, minor judgments, and ruses he needs to argue with his wife, or something of that sort, and it takes him countless attempts to get there?—You, young friend and author of an important sociological treatise, approach an influential patron. You enter his study, feeling sure of your significance, the lofty worth of your pursuit, the excellence of your achievement. But lo and behold! Your posturing is reduced to a low level of groveling, your rapid breathing robs your voice of the proper intonation and the requisite chest resonance. Your gestures are feeble and unconvincing. In short, you're simply not in a position to present yourself, to breathe life credibly into your presentation, you're fascinated and riveted by the superb sweeping motion with which your impressive destiny reaches for the needed mouthpiece, and in the ensuing pause, you lose your train of thought to analytical ideas about the nature of this greatness instead of keeping your own machinery in order. Nervousness? No, friend! Ignorance! Obliviousness! You simply ought to have learned it.—Where?— That's the problem. . . .

Isn't it really deeply shameful, even downright inexplicable, that in the era of scientific approaches to advertising, of experimental and psychological job testing, and all other Americanizing achievements in seamless life management, each individual is still forced to learn firsthand, over time, what could have been conveyed in a single year of systematic instruction in matters of tones of voice, catchphrases, arm movements, and facial gestures? And there he stands, bloated with life experience, as these ludicrous yet indispensable trifles are grandiosely labeled, with the sort of callousness of a boss who has no intention of sparing a trainee from any obstacles or the slightest failure. This approach to life is truly medieval, wallowing as it does in cumbersome dark insinuations, ominous prophesies, and pompous admonitions, instead of coming out and creating a school for things of this sort, teaching young people the art of swindling in an exciting and lively manner. What a gain in time! What a gain in vitality! And how simple the setup of this new discipline; all it would entail would be a study of physiognomy, human typology, plus a little instruction in conflicts, drama, and vocal exercises.—"Today we are coming to the subject of indignation" will—we hope—be what a teacher says in class in the not-too-distant future. "In the last class, we learned how to accept ingratiating praise, and we're now moving on to indignation and the three practical forms it can take. Lederer, give us a short summary of what we've learned!"—And Lederer, in his seventeenth year of life, will step forward, and with the most magnificent ease, smoothly and unhesitatingly, present the eight or ten words and gestures that we, now forty years old, can barely stammer out without focusing every fiber of our being each time we have to do it. "Very good, Lederer," the teacher will say, "just make your voice a little deeper. Make the movement of your hand toward the floor somewhat more pronounced, and slow down the whole thing by two seconds." And one will progress to the three kinds of indignation, greeting techniques, disdainful posturing, and communicating with the authorities and eventually bring the final phase of the course to a successful conclusion with the difficult but vital topic of self-promotion.

Berliner Börsen Courier, May 1, 1927

Naphthalene

It started on Tuesday. The landlady, a retired circus rider, with astounding bowlegs and a silver brooch with a horse head, whip, and horseshoe arranged in a most delightful way, came into my room and walked past me wordlessly. I'm saying "wordlessly," because I am not willing to interpret as words the French mumbling that got caught in the bits of her graying mustache and of which I understood only the word *printemps*.

In a flash she had opened the double window. I wanted to register strong protest. But the draft coming in from the courtyard lifted my unpaid bill for April from the desk, then it fluttered for a while between the still life with tomatoes and the dusty floor lamp, until it fell right next to the calendar, just where the zero of the date was. (It was May 10.) So I didn't say anything. I just stuck my index finger, which was blue from the cold, into my mouth and put my letter to Olive into an envelope, placed the April bill as a bookmark into the Jack London, took my hat from the hook, and left.

The hallway carried a distinct smell of oil. The landlady, her cousin, and the maid were standing in front of a huge open suitcase. With growing enthusiasm they were cramming whole piles of carpets, old clothing, and stuffed animals into the suitcase. The landlady herself commanded every movement, in her right hand she held a bag out of which she dumped some sort of white powder over the whole *chose*, the way confectioners' sugar is poured over pancakes. I came closer and saw the women embalming my coat. At the same time it occurred to me that this obnoxious confectioners' sugar bore the name *naphthalene*. Let them do so, I thought, and went to the café.

On Wednesday at 11:30 on the dot I sneezed three times. At Aschinger's I left over half of my bockwurst and got my next-to-last handkerchief from home. I took my umbrella along, too. At Wittenbergplatz I thought I heard hail pounding on the pavement. And my coat took on the smell of naphthalene, far away, in the suitcase and on the floor.

Thursday. Hans brought me a thermometer: 103.2, not bad at all. I gargle with saltwater, they wrap their cousin's wool stocking around my neck. The maid has been washing

handkerchiefs since breakfast. My hot eyes see only the three
Ice Saints, Mamertus, Pancras, and Servatius, juggling moth-
balls right next to my bed. Through the door in the hallway a
stupid smell of oil seems to be penetrating once again. I think
they're unpacking.

Berliner Börsen Courier, May 13, 1927

Anything but Objectivity!

To the linguist interested in human communication, the little
word "but" appears in an interesting light. From the outset—
and everyone will readily agree with me on this—its function
is to coyly introduce hitches into the smooth course of things
and to kill off the hope created by the words "I would love
to . . ." with candied poison. But then—and here I'll want to
step into more intellectual territory—the word "but" is the rep-
rehensible vehicle of an unhealthy objectivity, especially when
it comes to judging people. How often have even I replied to
the remark by a friend that one person or another was a preten-
tious schmuck by declaring, "But he studied philosophy with
Georg Simmel" and thus flung myself into the arms of an objectivity that unnecessarily complicates the world in a manner
that bedevils life, plunges the mind into dilemmas, kills the im-
pulse to act, and on top of that has the appalling effect of surrounding us, anywhere and everywhere, with interesting people.

The few true connoisseurs of the art of living among you
know the sensual pleasure of calling someone an ass or cretin,
plain and simple, without being constrained later to remark on
how splendidly he plays the piano and thus undermine what
you've said; of pronouncing an awkward person simply unbearable without needing to declare afterward that she is basically

a shy soul with terrible inhibitions. Anything but objectivity! It unsettles your heart, makes your character fickle and ambivalent, and anyone who uses it excessively sooner or later descends into severe neurosis, as if an emotion had been jammed into you.

The public, our blessed public, doesn't have this objectivity and is in excellent health. It knows how to invoke forceful words full of vivid imagery, fierce statements toward disagreeable individuals, apodictic judgments that by their very nature don't allow for any ensuing "buts." Even the most objective person couldn't come up with a way to tone down a statement like calling someone a "monumental jackass," making it seem as though the person thus characterized nonetheless has a good grasp of the subtlest stylistic nuances. Statements of this kind coming from straightforward, forthright individuals have the unassailable nature of mathematical axioms—a priori ideas are just there, not amenable to any explanation, any refutation, like mountains made of glass.

Actions like taking a dainty bow or turning the toes outward when walking gracefully, like harmful objectivity, stem from the world of courtly life, which provided the model for urban culture over the course of centuries. Objectivity was the virtue of a good monarch, was the benevolent ruler's compassion for the weaknesses and strengths of his subjects, was the onset, the primordial cell of a democratic form of government that grants even the minority the right to throw in a word as they please, and that later, at around the close of the nineteenth century, reached its heyday with the catchwords "On one hand, on the other hand!" and "But still . . . !"

It seems only natural that in accordance with the march of history, so-called democracy always makes a point of contrasting itself with dictatorship, which leads to a change in the arena of personal objectivity; in short, that the fretful dithering when pronouncing judgment about this one or that one ultimately puts a stop to people cheerfully, heartily, and vigorously granting absolute validity to their judgments, as in a dictatorship, and returning to the method of nature, to an unspoiled, healthy populace from which all power emanates, and calling a nitwit a nitwit with a clear conscience even if he really does write the very loveliest couplets. Ruthless dictatorship of judgment is what I am pushing for. You should no longer be mentally constrained to acknowledge the undeniable virtues of a friend whose very approach from a distance turns your stomach. Think of your health! Back to the good, irrefutable, utterly fresh swear words our people so richly have at their command. Out with the word that's on the tip of your tongue. Anything but objectivity!

Berliner Börsen Courier, May 20, 1927

When It's Eighty-four Degrees

The thermometer has hit eighty-four degrees. Not because anyone has been holding a match under the mercury bulb, but in an altogether natural way, as some long-awaited high or low pressure system has invaded us. Yesterday people were boasting that even the most extreme desert temperatures would be a pleasure compared to this cold, damp, unsettled weather. Now they have the pleasure. So much for that. Ice water on your head, ice water into your stomach. A bit of a headache and stomachache. Where do you hole up on this uselessly free afternoon? An attack of tropical madness. Let's go all out. People head off to the five o'clock tea dance.

And—this is no mirage, but the reality of Berlin—others who've been driven mad by the heat are already here. Easily a few dozen, male and female. Sitting in front of their iced sodas feeling boiling hot. They let the summer come at them and valiantly do their duty. The saxophone attacks the opening jazz number. Everyone's in place to dance the Black Bottom. When it's eighty-four degrees. With admirable energy, though not exactly setting speed records, the couples shimmy their way through the long oval. Subdued applause. The second round. Every now and then a leg refuses to engage in this activity, which is properly performed in the winter. The smarter dancers are glued to their spots, with just a hint of swinging. Today there are none of the usual handshakes from the lady, only a parting smile. She slings a silk scarf over her forehead, takes a swig from the yellow straw; the next dance.

At the window the oppressive heat grows unbearable. And by God, the dancers seem to feel better. Perhaps it is not at all that preposterous to drive out the devil's heat with the Black Bottom. They jump in, eyes closed.

"The man at the drums slipped up on his instrument." The woman with the bright-green silk scarf, whom I've asked to dance and is now fluttering marvelously in front of me, ignores my cultivated sense of hearing. Her withering glance tells me that one doesn't dishonor the Black Bottom by speaking. Of course. But, needing to come out with something again, I add to my words of wisdom: "Every dilettante has a go at the drum. It actually takes some training. I myself . . ." Then an unexpected burst of light startles me. Embarrassing mistake. That wasn't a blunder on the part of the drummer, but instead a gently rising rumble of thunder—here comes another flash of lightning—a real thunderstorm. My Little Miss Silk also realizes what's going on, to her horror, suddenly flutters closer, turns downright approachable. The bluish-black sky appears menacing through the windows. The blazing light bulbs do nothing to offset the looming threat. The thunder keeps getting more fearsome, the bolts of lightning eerier. The band competes heroically with the sounds of nature, but it can't stop the Black Bottom from degenerating into a frantic slide.

I lead my crumpled Little Miss Silk to her seat. She stares at the storm in silence. In order not to disturb her with loud parting words, I occupy the chair next to her. Endless minutes of nothing but thunder and lightning. I place my unsightly pocket watch on the table and examine the second hand. "Sound travels at the speed of 1,125 feet per second. The storm can't be far off." All of a sudden, Little Miss Silk's face contorts with fear but still bears the look of a sweet young girl. "By the way, my Fräulein, we are on the second floor, that is, on the top floor of this building." *Don't look, don't move*, I order myself. "Since this building hasn't been around for long, it may not have a lightning rod yet."

Enough. The last clap of thunder isn't even needed. With a final scream she jumps up, tries to cling to my arm. I throw my rain poncho over her and convey Elli to safety, as a savior deserving of her gratitude, in a nearby bar on the ground floor.

Please, please, another storm tomorrow.

Berliner Börsen Courier, June 1, 1927

Day of Destiny

Under today's date, across the page, the space reserved for comments in my pocket calendar says: *Day of destiny*. Underlined twice. An unusual choice of vocabulary for a notepad. Apart from that, the entire page has only names and numbers. Yesterday there were reminders to pay my bills, and for Pentecost, a list of train connections and hotels. And then this solemn note. And yet this is undeniably my own entry; even the double emphasis was in my handwriting. I start to recall.

It happened about three weeks ago. After a long time I was able to take a relaxing afternoon stroll once again, with window-shopping on Tauentzienstrasse. Suddenly, at Wittenbergplatz, shouts and laughter from a surging crowd of people. Leader or victim, in the center with wild gestures, is a pale youth, his bloodless lips spread wide for a scream, barely aware of the disparaging heckling, as he hurls out his indictment of "this era, which has grown heartless." Very softly, audible only to those standing closest to him, he ends up with: "But the fourth of June will be the day of destiny for all." How so? He can't, and won't, say. Still, as if sensing the dreadfulness to come, a shudder runs over his body as he names the date.

Then he begins the second part of his tirade. The policeman on the corner stares indifferently at the speaker, whose words are turning more and more impassioned. "He has the paragraph in his pocket," someone explains.

So today is the day of destiny. For us all. I don't consider this type of prophecy the end of the world, even if it's tied to a specific day. But now that I'm reminded of it, I do feel obliged to be a little attentive. I find myself thinking of it as I open the mail, or read the latest telegrams. Nothing out of the ordinary has happened. Natural catastrophes—bloody confrontations—accidents—a flight across the ocean. It's sure to be fateful for many, but not for everyone. There is no hint of an earthshaking event. But now I'm overcome with major misgivings about whether it is at all possible to take stock of this day right now, even just concerning the significance, or insignificance, of an incident. Anything can start out unrecognizably, anything can turn into a dire fate. I realize how flippant I'm being. All at once everything becomes important and serious.

How would it be if, for just one day, *everyone* all of a sudden were to regard everything as important and serious? The mechanized sequence of their family life, the pattern underlying their professional work. Saying good morning to their wives, signing documents.—Day of destiny?

Berliner Börsen Courier, June 4, 1927

Wanted: Perfect Optimist

AN IMAGINARY DISPATCH FROM
NEW YORK CITY

April 14. I read this announcement in today's *New York Herald:*

> Wanted:
> Short, fat man with a bald head and good teeth. Forty dollars a week.
> Come tomorrow between eight and ten.
> Gridgeman,
> Marmalade wholesale, 293 Ninth Street.

April 15. I was the first. Mister Gridgeman looked over my physique, examined my bald head and teeth, then said, "Smile." I didn't quite understand, and he repeated his request. The situation was so odd that I found it a little hard to start grinning from ear to ear. "So, you're hired." Mister Gridgeman clapped me on the back with a hand as hard as steel. We went into his private office. He pointed to a leather chair right across from his desk. "Your task will be to sit in this armchair every day from eight to two. You can read detective stories, write memoirs, smoke, even darn socks for all I care. But you have to smile, and keep on smiling. That's the essential thing. Forty dollars a week. And you start tomorrow. Goodbye."

April 16. I have a sleepless night behind me. This Mister Gridgeman seems to be insane. Or does he want to showcase me to his customers, claiming that my corpulence comes solely from my regular indulgence in the unrivaled Gridgeman marmalade?—I'm right in place at eight on the dot. Mister

Gridgeman is already there. I sit down. I start my work a bit bashfully. I smile over at Mister Gridgeman. Here and there I look around me. Highly instructive statistics about the protein content of California plums and some ten clever sayings are mounted on the walls, praising Gridgeman bananas as skyscrapers of goodness, nutritional value, and culture. Also: What perfume could be finer than the aroma of our pineapple jam?— Through the glass door I see the nice slim face of a typist with straight black hair, typing at a good pace and making a rather good impression on me.—I smile the whole time, two hours, four hours, six hours.

April 22. This is a splendid job. They've paid me my first weekly wages, forty dollars. I think that, given my preposterous work, I am the best-paid guy on the planet.—Mister Gridgeman hasn't said a word to me yet about the whys and wherefores. My curiosity dies down. I have thought through all the possibilities and didn't come up with much. Mister Gridgeman is just a harmless madman, and I don't have the guts to ask a madman questions. Incidentally, Mister Gridgeman is very kind to me. I smoke his cigars and chew his gum. When he's dictating business letters to the nice typist—her name is Bessie—he gives me a friendly nod. During his long-distance telephone calls to Philadelphia, Baltimore, and Denver, and to the plantations in Alabama and South Carolina, he returns my smile. And when businesspeople come, he introduces me to them as a friend. He provides price quotes, talks about the new harvest and about his superb grapefruits, and receives orders for his marmalade by the truckload. But not for a second does he look away from my eyes and my lips, which are frozen in an everlasting smile.

May 4. Everything is going along swimmingly. I got bad news from Jefferson City: my in-laws' farm was severely affected by the catastrophic flooding of the Mississippi. But that won't stop me from keeping a smile on my face.

May 7. Mister Gridgeman seems to be quite satisfied with me. His hard-as-steel hand claps me on the shoulder more and more often; I already have a good dozen black-and-blue marks. Every day I am served ice cream at midday. My wages have been raised to fifty dollars. On Sunday, Bessie and I will go to a base-ball game.

May 17. I'm feeling quite glum; Bessie has suddenly gotten engaged to an underwear manufacturer in the Bronx. What should I do? I have to smile. Maybe this'll do the trick: I've subscribed to satirical magazines, *Life*, *Punch*, the *New Yorker*, and the *Judge*. But I think that's the wrong way to go about it. I'd rather read the political section of the daily newspapers.

May 31. Gridgeman has sealed a very big deal. He bursts into loud laughter, comes up to me, and hits me on the shoulder so hard that I sink to my knees. "Well, now! You are a great guy; you got me customers for my entire inventory of marmalade, and I bet that 80 percent of it was moldy. It was a fine idea to hire you. Ah, you don't even know yet what I need you for. You are my lucky charm. I have to have an optimist around me, a fat guy who is always laughing and reflects life. When I see you, nothing can go wrong, nothing."

June 1. Today I found the office door barred and the lock sealed by the authorities. Under the company's nameplate was a small strip of paper with the typed message: "Closed down for bankruptcy by the courts."

Berliner Börsen Courier, July 3, 1927

Renovation

AN ODE TO THE COFFEEHOUSE

Coffeehouses have something in common with well-played violins. They resonate, reverberate, and impart distinct timbres. The many years of the regular guests' clamor have amassed their filaments and atoms in a singular way, and the woodwork, paneling, and even pieces of furniture pulse marvelously to the tunes of the visitors' life rhythms. Malice and venomous thoughts of a decade on the blackened walls have settled in as a sweetly radiant finish, as the finest patina. Every sound, emanating from the faintest quiver, the most unremarkable brains, comes through and runs endlessly, in mysterious waves, across all the molecules of the magnificently played sound body, day after day, with the regulars playing the strings to attain the uplifting resonance that their lives, professions, or families generally fail to deliver. The molecular miracle that unfolds here, the phenomenon of metaphysical ensoulment of favorite pubs from the aura of their guests, has yet to be the subject of scholarly research.

But would it ever occur to any owner of an Amati violin to use sandpaper to scrub off the vintage, resounding finish of his instruments, the atoms of which are filled and fulfilled by the sonority of countless concerts, and coat the violin with fine gold bronze? This deplorable barbarity is being increasingly deployed to carry out a procedure of this sort in people's favorite pubs! One day you go into the old familiar place and find the furniture gone, and you catch sight of men on high ladders with taunting paper caps using sharp tools to scrape your most precious essences and deposits off the walls. To your dismay you make out the best joke of your life, now reduced to fine dust

along those walls, along with the uproarious laughter it occa-
sioned, and you stumble across the apt remarks you once made
about the nature of chess fans, and you're standing there just as
the lavatory attendant, taken away temporarily from her other
duties, uses a rag to wipe up the tender words from the floor
that you whispered in Amalie's ears in 1916, and—with minor
adjustments—Laura's in 1918. His head tilted to size up the
matter, his hand on his watch chain, the coffeehouse owner
stands at my side, while I'm deeply moved, and says, "There!
Have a look!"

So, now it's going to be different. Somewhere there are two
beautiful elephant heads with torch-bearing trunks, to be used
as tasteful lighting ornaments for the two pillars. A family of
fishermen, roof tiles from Lake Gosau, and farmers' girls in
richly carved Renaissance frames are awaiting their decorative
destinations. Red and gold. Brocade and repp. The dancer Kitty
Starling . . . a polar bear prowling around a block of ice bathed
in light . . .

It's the women's fault, believe me, women with their horri-
bly deficient sense of history, which manifests itself in such a
blessedly disastrous manner as a love of tidiness and cleanli-
ness; women with their endearing attachment to the present,
paying no heed to the stream of time, but instead focusing
determinedly on countering the passage of eons with cosmet-
ics, apparel, and beating carpets. Their efforts are aimed at
demolishing time. When would a man ever get the idea of
repainting a foyer? When would a painter ever have imagined
that the paintbrush in his practiced hand was a close relative
of the powder puff standing up to the pyramids at Giza? But
when, on the other hand, did a woman ever fully grasp the
metaphysical outlook of the man that stops him from giving
away his old hats, perched as they are atop his thoughts, or
tossing them away, willy-nilly?

Blindly carrying over her ideals to venerable taverns, which are steeped in tradition, she is eager, as the wife of a coffeehouse proprietor, to enforce the principle of domesticity in the café as well as at home, doing a thorough job of it, tidying up, painting, in short, obliterating time and providing a squeaky-clean, cozy home for the guest. But, I ask you, who actually looks forward to heading home? She pressures her reluctant spouse to go with the times, remodel, alter the image, gild the place, add red, polish the furniture, and dye the pub's hair.

The local pub, a site of extreme masculinity, is about to acquire an utterly feminine aspect that lends the concept of "passing the time" an odd and quite specifically feminine slant with tireless renovation and beaming disavowal of all the years gone by. Revered countenance of everyone's favorite bar! With gold and red, time has been driven out of your features. The regular visitor is appalled by the destruction of his years, by the eradication of the bits of himself he has breathed into the place. But the woman in charge has taken on a new coffeehouse . . .

Berliner Börsen Courier, July 13, 1927

Why Don't Matches Smell That Way Anymore?

I woke up at night. The rain beat against the windowpanes. A thin gleam slid across the wall. Someone had turned on a light in the building across the street, and at this moment it came my way. It was not merely a sensation of smell that took hold of me, it was more of an almost painful feeling rushing through my whole body, permeating every cell, and transforming it in some mysterious way.

So, how was it?

Well, it was like this: a match whooshed gently across the striking surface, and light blazed up. And silently, eerily, the blue spirits' flame arose. Its fragrance blended with the last trace of the dying match. Now the aroma of a sweet hint of cocoa was added on, with a slow hum as it warmed. What was this wonderful symphony of scents that was suddenly caressing and cajoling my face? What sort of voices were these? . . . Spirits . . . cocoa. . . . extinguishing match . . . Why don't matches smell like that anymore?

Yes, how has that happened? Have development, progress, catastrophe left their mark on you, too, you matches? Is it a yearning for something new, or the lack of time, that forms you from different, cold materials today? Your soul is gone. Do you have a new one? I don't get that sense. Am I too old to capture the spirit of things with eager nostrils the way I once did?

Oh, blessed fragrance from the sun-kissed leather cushions of a carriage! The sun was baking, thin, fine dust lay on the street, and dried grass gave off its scent, green and herbaceous, up from the ground. The Corpus Christi procession had passed by here. There were whipcords. Stepping into the little shop, you would see them hanging there at the door by the dozens, dark, slender worms adorned with colored little woolen tassels, black and new, and emitting a fragrance that signified horse and stable and mighty rule over both. And out of one of the countless drawers that rose all the way up to the ceiling came the pervasive aroma of a singular, mysterious spice that had never been granted to any mortal being in the clientele's circle to see, to feel, to put a name to. Enticing to young people wishing to enter the store three times a day, a trade secret revealed only to its greatest luminaries. They knew how to guard this secret well. If I asked, they explained, with duplicitous looks on their faces, that they didn't know what I meant. Expensive smells. "Whipcord" and "general store," what's become of you?

And then: First day in the summer apartment. Scent of wet terra alba used to paint the staircase bright white. A musty, gritty smell arose from the cellar. Added to this enchanting duality was a mixture of polish and winter apples coming from the rooms. Oh, it was dazzling!—Swim class, that was like the smell of a new rubber ball, hot gray wood and paper to which some butter, softened by the sun, was still stuck. The hothouse was moist, wet earth, a site of silence. The silence had its fragrance as well. Even the air smelled so delightful on some winter days! What component of coal might that have been? There were three kinds of aromas at play. I called them "Song Without Words," "Sonate Pathétique," and "Mums." Today, I think, coal comes from Silesia, and it just smells like coal. Silesian coal is neutral. Back then it may have been coal from Cardiff. Maybe in England it still smells like "Song Without Words."

The light on the wall has gone out. I turn to the other side.— Lost! I say. They use new materials. During the war they ran out of many materials, which were replaced by different, cheaper ones. Now people are staying with them. That is progress. A world has disappeared and will never, ever come back. From an economic standpoint it is not important for the winter air to smell like "Sonate Pathétique." Dried grass is referred to as hay. It is cattle fodder. Phosphorus can no longer be used to make matches.

Someday I may well get to Paris and in the central warehouse of the famed perfume factory inquire about the lost and lovely inspiring "Astris." The old salesman will leaf through a catalog. "Oh, Sir," he will say, "we stopped making that a long time ago. An older perfume. It's no longer in demand."—And with the sound of these words the appearance of that beloved being will vanish for good, holding his bathrobe high over his radiant head, wading through the shallow sea over to the island.—"You are sad, Sir," the salesman will say. "We perfumers have a sad profession. We kill the past. Perfumes pass on, and so do their worlds. . . . And we create new ones again."

"This bottle"—and he will show me a sparkling, spraying little crystal bottle—"our latest creation, *L'avenir*—what destiny, do you think, might lie dormant here?—We're a bit godlike, aren't we? No, perhaps it's not so sad to be a perfumer after all."

And I will ask him warily: "Do you know the scent of the cellar stairs? Or perhaps the smell of the dying match? Whipcord? Swimming pool? Why, Sir, always the future? Why everything to the young? Why anticipation? Why not memory? *Parfums retrospectives*! *Escalier de cave; Cordelette de fouet; Petit nageur; Allumette mourante* . . . I ask you—"

He gazes at me. His good bearded face blurs, and I fall asleep.

Berliner Börsen Courier, August 10, 1927

The Rose of Jericho

This miracle has existed, you might say, since "biblical" times. The prophet Jeremiah mentions the Rose of Jericho in a variety of contexts. In the quest for new export products, the Palestinian export trade has now brought this attraction to us as well. For two marks, everyone can now purchase this mysterious plant in fine flower shops. About the size of a pear, dirty yellow in color, its small dried-up leaves scrunched together, this scrawny moss might not even be regarded as a "flower" at all. But, as so often in life, appearances are deceiving. In *boiling* water this Cinderella undergoes a miraculous metamorphosis. With this flower, an otherwise lethal process turns life-giving, and the botanical monstrosity blossoms into the Rose of Jericho.

Overwhelmed by scientific curiosity, I sacrificed two marks and bought the plant. In the afternoon I visited Steffie. I got there as she was making coffee, as she was about to pour the boiling water. "Stop," I cried, "watch this: a miracle will now take place." I pulled the hidden Rose of Jericho out of my jacket pocket and tossed it into the coffeepot. Steffie and I watched intensely for quite a while. Roughly an hour. Then it slowly happened. The dirty yellow transformed into dark green, the small, dried leaves began to spread apart. It was certainly quite nice, but it would take the authority of a prophet to pass off this high school physics experiment as a "miracle."

The next day I brought my rose back to the flower shop. "Miss," I complained to the saleswoman, "I don't like your miracle. Please exchange it for me." Since there was no other miracle on hand, I settled for a cactus. A cactus always comes in handy. For instance, the thirtieth of the month was Aunt Emma's birthday. Seven years earlier I had presented her a silver-plated pencil I found in the subway. Since then that unfortunate date had not permitted me to buy any more birthday presents. This time I will delight her with the prickly plant. "But, my boy," she'll say, "you have money for a present on the thirtieth? Will wonders never cease?"—Which goes to show that the Rose of Jericho at least indirectly confirmed the quality ascribed to it.

Berliner Börsen Courier, August 19, 1927

Little Economics Lesson

Thirty-five years ago, I was given a present of a children's chocolate vending machine. You would beg your relatives desperately for money, throw it into the machine, give one pull—and right in front of the buyer or seller, a bar of chocolate would appear, turning gray at the edges, and it was happily offered to your aunt. When the machine was empty, it could be opened with a little key, and the available money had to be used to purchase new supplies, which in bulk came out somewhat cheaper than getting them from a vending machine. In addition to having a toy to play with, you also got a nice little lesson in the workings of a supply chain. You earned profits, replenished your inventory, and functioned as an entrepreneur. "Business personified," in the guise of a fairy-tale prince, peered into the nursery through a crack in the door. It was there that sales prowess was trained from an early age, pushiness perfected, and business sense aroused and placed in the service of national wealth.

The chocolate vending machine was the model. It's hard to grasp that it took until now for the seed planted in me so far in the past to sprout; just recently this productive idea has ripened, an idea I am now preparing to implement to make myself rich and powerful. "Each his own middleman" is the motto by which I now intend to live and whose meaning and contents I hereby convey to the public.

One example: I shave my own face. I buy soap, brush, styptic pencil, aftershave, and powder. I sharpen the knives. I spend time, effort, and money on removing my beard neatly. What use do I get out of that? Where do the capital revenues and output of my daily efforts wind up? Has it ever crossed my mind, in all my heedlessness, to remunerate myself appropriately for all my labor? A criminal waste of economic capital! From now on this will be different. I will pay myself. I will shave my face a bit more cheaply than the guy who does shaves, because I'll want to compete with him. *But I'll pay myself.*

I'll give myself food that I'll buy at cheap prices and pass along to myself more expensively. How happy I will be to pocket the profit that the restaurant gets for a couple of sausages!

For all the necessities of life that I fulfill for myself as an entrepreneur, I'll add a middleman surcharge of 20 percent to the cost of the goods and services.

I'll get my chewing gum from a vending machine set up in my hallway, and the profit will go straight to me.

I'll get myself cigarettes for no more than the price that waiters charge.

When I unlock the front door I'll give myself a tip.

I'll constantly court myself as a consumer for whom only the very best will do, and to whom demonstrating the greatest obligingness is one of my immutable business principles.

In my apartment are posters that employ sumptuous and invigorating words to tout the high quality of cosmetic items, the beneficial nature of well-established wine and liquor brands, and the effectiveness of tried-and-true medicines.

I'll prudently regulate supply and demand, constantly increase consumption with well-considered methods, and conduct effective advertising.

On a lectern there is a thick, bulky ledger in which I note down my business dealings under debit and credit with the meticulousness of a shrewd businessman. I take stock daily. I know at all times what I need to achieve.

Unfortunately, I am somewhat lacking in working capital. Recently I gathered some information about myself from Schimmelpfeng. Should I continue to extend myself credit? As a businessman, I need to exercise caution.

I fear I'm not looking good.

Berliner Börsen Courier, August 21, 1927

Film Terror

ON THE THREAT OF BEING PHOTOGRAPHED

This has been going on for months already, twice a day, at noon on the way to the restaurant, and barely an hour later when I come back, always at the same inevitable spot, this person harasses me, ambushes me as he calls out his solemn, menacing message: *You have just been filmed.* The first few times, I was seriously frightened, and actually thought that some director on the hunt for characters had chosen me without my knowledge to play an extra. Now that I know this nonsense has nothing to do with the world of movies, only a modern new type of business that represents "action photography," I'm less thin-skinned about it. Even so, the formulation of this statement, this insulting passive "being filmed," never ceases to bother me.

It rankles me that without even obtaining my consent, this picture-hungry yellow box can keep taking possession of my face, even though I go to great pains to avoid appearing in front of any camera lens. But what annoys me even more than this intrusion is actually the blind idiocy of the cameraman, this witless wastrel who went to great effort a hundred times to capture my portrait, a hundred times in vain sent his leaflet distributor to get me, but still failed to recognize my aversion to film every time, and still inflicts on me twice a day the unpleasant duty of leaving him disappointed. I tried with various demonstrations, holding my hat in front of my head, looking toward the other side of the street, waving him aside with my arms and hands, but nothing works—the cameraman interpreted everything as just a new and interesting variant of his action studies.

Recently I thought I could escape my fate by choosing a side street beyond the range of the camera. But I hadn't counted on the tripod being mobile, and all it took was a little rotation to catch up with me on my escapade.

After giving the matter quite a bit of thought, I have now tried an experiment that I hope will free me from the film terror once and for all. Not grudgingly, offering opposition as I had in the past, no, smiling gleefully, with a stiff posture, eyes right to the camera, really photography-friendly, I allowed myself to be filmed, then gratefully received the announcement of my film premiere.

Yesterday I picked up my picture. My legs seemed somewhat overly crooked—most likely a problem with the lens—but other than that it was a very lifelike, moving photograph. Under the photograph I wrote in red ink, "This person no longer wishes to be filmed," and handed it to the cameraman at noon. "You see," I explained to him, "it would be best for you to attach this picture directly to your camera. If you do that, you'll save a filmstrip every day and I can finally go into my restaurant undisturbed." He seemed too astonished at my offer to come up with a reply on the spot. I don't seriously think he'll fulfill my wish, but even so, he will surely remember my face. That someone does not pick up his picture is something he understands, from his everyday experience, as a reflection of financial inertia. But the idea that someone would forfeit payment of a mark in order *not* to be filmed is ultimately a thinly veiled attack on his *professional honor*. Something of that sort is not forgotten. I hope he doesn't now come up with the idea of launching a new business in— film removal.

Berliner Börsen Courier, September 1, 1927

Berlin Rendezvous

Rendezvous *(Fr., pronounced raan-dey-voo, "present yourselves"): a meetup, together, at a specific spot, also the place itself.*

Adam, for example, liked to meet up with Eve at a certain apple tree. As for Ramses, he waited patiently every single evening at the third corner of the twelfth pyramid for his favorite lady. Caesar, by contrast, met up with Vercingetorix in the rain under the Rhine Bridge. The excesses in which Casanova indulged cannot be described in view of space limitations; his rendezvous are said to have been recorded in a saffiano leather tome as thick as a Berlin telephone book.

There are distinctions between rendezvous pertaining to business, friendship, love, and family; consequently, there are rendezvous that people are happy to go to and others they dread.

Rendezvous at apple trees, pyramids, and under Rhine bridges have naturally fallen out of fashion. Nowadays people prefer to use a café, a restaurant for these purposes. People meet up outdoors, at popular gathering spots, under monuments and clocks, at streetcar stops, and in front of theaters and cinema houses.

In Berlin, three places are the top choices: the Kranzlerecke, that famous street corner on Kurfürstendamm; the Berolina on Alexanderplatz; and the Normaluhr, the oversized clock, at the Zoo railway station. (This does not claim to be a complete list.)

As far as the *Kranzlerecke* is concerned, it vividly recalls one of the world's classic meeting points, the Sirkecke in Vienna. It is the rendezvous spot for international society, the gathering place of the glamorous set that is at home in the hotels on Unter den Linden. Madame sports a chinchilla fur and doesn't wait for too long; her pinscher looks around for Monsieur and barks.

Mustaches carry the fragrance of Paris pomades, every trouser crease is absolutely precise, and the honking cars sound like a well-rehearsed saxophone concert. Berliners get together there too, of course, but rarely, usually to go to the theater or to amble through the museum in the evening: midtown Berlin.

Alexanderplatz is the rendezvous spot for the stream of women in the workforce—civil servants and shopgirls—who move along until the plaza and jam up at the bus stops and the subway. There, a young woman waits. Determinedly. He has to come. She'll wait three more minutes, and if he doesn't come then . . . He doesn't come. The girl decides to count to a hundred. Counts up to nine hundred. Not a trace of him. It is well past the fifteen-minute mark. I'm going to strangle him, she tells herself. Then he comes. And arm in arm they flutter away.

The most popular summer rendezvous point is the *Normal-uhr* at the Zoo railway station. The gateway to nature. Packed with families on Sundays. Kith and kin. Sunday drivers. Juveniles. Boy scouts. Country bumpkins with badges at their buttonholes. A date for the Wannsee. Or for the Kurfürstendamm Kino. Or for five o'clock tea. For the amusement park. Or for the zoo. Everyone stares up at the clock. Sometimes it goes so fast, sometimes so slow. But there are also rendezvous that are *not* kept.

Why, it occurred to me, would I choose the Tiergarten bench as a meeting point in this cold weather, where I waited for her in vain? And it didn't hail and it didn't rain.

Berliner Börsen Courier, November 13, 1927

Night Ride over Berlin

HOW GERMAN NIGHT FLIGHT OPERATIONS
ARE ORGANIZED

"But now I'm curious," said the neighbor to my left, as she pressed her nose against the ice-cold windowpane of the airplane cabin and looked down while we were passing by Schöneberg, "whether my husband is home yet." Fifteen minutes earlier she was still a bundle of nerves, freezing, her teeth chattering. She put up a brave front and tried to fool all of us while facing the roaring three-engine plane, then refreshed her lipstick, which rendered her lips as signal red as the neon tubes that bordered the Tempelhof field.

Well, as we flew over Berlin, with one curve after another, at night at an altitude of two thousand feet, all nine passengers fell for her composure, even for the straightforward consideration she showed for her husband in Schöneberg, which she displayed clear as day or, rather, clear as night.

After all, how did we really feel? Cool to our very hearts.

And what was below us? The sea of lights of Berlin.

How were the motors working? Like precision instruments. What lay behind us? The concerns of an incredulous generation. And in front of us, any moment now, Bal paré in the giant aircraft, followed by a billiards tournament. The development is that rapid.

Because today even the night is a time for traffic.

In 1924, when we heard that American airship travel had instituted regular day-and-night service between New York and San Francisco, we shook our heads in disbelief. We had yet to be convinced of the safety of a daytime flight, and technical futurists were already planning to do everything they could not to waste the night, the terribly dark, perilous night: to fly independent of time, irrespective of whether land could be sighted below.

People are not drawn to fly at night for the sport of it; the impetus for nighttime travel arises from the need to travel great distances. The seasons, the winter, even the fall and the spring make it necessary to fly after dark as well. We no longer wish to sacrifice the day to travel; it is part of work.

Germany was ahead of all the other European countries in the arena of nighttime travel. In 1924 the Berlin–Warnemünde–Stockholm route was used for overnight airmail, and Berlin–Copenhagen and Berlin–Hamburg followed. The year 1926 saw the first nighttime passenger flights along the Berlin–Königsberg route as a link in the London–Moscow air route. In the course of the past few years, airports, routes, and the airplanes themselves have been adapted to accommodate night duty. Light signals were introduced, wind direction indicators were added, and landing areas were surrounded with floodlights that illuminated large areas in green and white and red. They even went to the length of compensating for the reduced visibility compared to daytime flying by constructing a row of lights with a high-wattage rotating searchlight mounted every eighteen miles, and prominent neon lamps every three miles. These light towers are in service night after night, all indicating emergency landing fields. But that's not something to think about right off; a carefully devised system of signals, the use of radio telegraphy, landing lights, and magnesium lighting on the wings of the planes ensure the same level of safety as during the day. The pilots are all experienced veterans, and it is regarded as a special distinction to serve as a night pilot.

Director Milch, who gave these explanations yesterday during an official visit to the nighttime illumination of the Tempelhof airfield, remarked in closing that the comprehensive implementation of aviation on all routes by day and by night was one of the most important tasks of international airship travel. In the foreseeable future we will easily work with all routes independent of the time of day and the weather conditions.

The Berlin–Hanover route has already been completed, as has the one linking Berlin and Königsberg. Berlin–Cologne, Berlin–Halle–Munich, and Berlin–Breslau are under construction, and in the spring new Junker airplanes will make it possible for Lufthansa to service all German routes at night as well.

The airplane glided over Berlin like a giant bat, giving people a clear view of the streets and squares of the city as they marveled at their ability to scan the enormous distance from the radio tower to the thermal power station in Rummelsburg at a glance. No sooner were we flying over the Kurfürstendamm than, after just one curve, the airplane was already rolling across the Tempelhof lawn. Seconds earlier, millions of lights had been shining up from below, but now there was nothing but night around us, and the airport building, which from above had seemed like a match, now towered up like a skyscraper.

Berliner Börsen Courier, December 6, 1927

The Business of Thirst

WHAT PEOPLE ARE DRINKING NOWADAYS

The saying about love and hunger making the world go round is quite literally wrong. These elemental factors should be named, but thirst is even more elemental, powerful, and immediate than hunger. There are people who can go hungry for two to six weeks, yet they can cope with thirst for forty-eight hours at most.

Hunger is a furious, burning sensation at first, then a weakness. A person's eagerness to satisfy hunger eases up, and the person is said to be too hungry to eat. Thirst is an opening up of the expectant body from deeper and deeper within, awaiting the moment when an overabundance of the long-anticipated drink streams into the dryness of the body.

Berlin has been dreaming of quenching thirst for days. Directly, with water, soda, beer, and ice cream, and indirectly (thirst of the skin), with baths, snow mountains, wind on a sailboat.

Heat renders manifest the most vital mystery of the body: we burn off moisture. The sun, which enables us to live, heightens its intensity: life, known in this form as sweat, breaks out. We dispense it to the atmosphere, we have to decompose. According to Joseph Löbl, perspiration amounts to ¾ quart per day even at moderate temperatures. Other numbers he cites: a ride through a southern Californian plain at 75 degrees produced 10½ quarts of sweat loss, an intense soccer game 14 pounds in 70 minutes, a marathon race 8½ pounds in three hours.

Berliners could now theoretically lose quite a bit of weight, free of charge! But they drink as much as their bodies can hold. Beer, with its thermal value, least of all. The spike in consumption is slight, as everyone knows that heat increases the debilitating effect of the beer. Let us recall that attempt at hiking the Bilkegrat. They climbed from 5,000 feet up to 8,000 feet, twice under the same conditions, but once after consuming an ounce of alcohol. Result: one-fifth more time = one-seventh greater energy consumption. Once this finding was expressed in popular terms, the result was a reduction of beer consumption in Germany, where it amounted to three quarts per capita, per week for every person over the age of fifteen in 1913, and by 1927 it was down to two quarts.

The big restaurants are even reporting a decline in beer consumption these days, offset by an increase in sparkling water and other carbonated drinks, and of course the sale of milk doesn't bring in much business. But at the bars, all the cocktails made with tea are selling better than ever.

Profiting the most from the heat are the small and makeshift drink stands and the train station restaurants. People quench their thirst when they get the chance; they don't arrange for it the way they do for a meal. Ice cream parlors and ice cream carts are showing the relatively highest sales increase. On Sundays, large snack bars geared to tourists have sold between four thousand and five thousand portions of ice cream, and small vending trucks up to five times the usual sales volume; they constantly need to restock their supplies. And all dining cars are sure to report as they reach their destination: "Drinks sold out."

But one day the unthinkable will come to pass once again: people will walk through the streets shivering, a winter breeze will rock back and forth a forgotten Iced Coffee sign at a shop door, and they will burrow their hands deeper into their pockets at the very sight of this sign.

B. Z. [*Berliner Zeitung*], July 18, 1928

Here We Are at Film Studio 1929

As is well known, the theater impresario Dr. Moriz Seeler has set up a film studio. At the beginning there was widespread enthusiasm, then disapproval came from the other side. Over on Friedrichstrasse, home of the banks and the moneymen, they were dying of laughter and placing their fingers on their carotid arteries while declaring: "If we find a sponsor for their project, we will stick an umbrella right in here!" Well, we have started, have happily received the money, and have been filming our crazy thing for ten days.

We get to work at a feverish pace. With a wobbly cart borrowed from a baker in Nikolassee, we drag the equipment across the sandy beach. Spend fourteen hours at the camera and tackle everything nicely. We hold the reflectors ourselves, kneel in the lake the whole day, and when we're on the verge of sunstroke, we just stick our heads in the water. I don't think the Chang or Pamir expeditions required more willpower and more deprivations. My God, we have such primitive resources on hand. A few miles down the road, on the premises of Neubabelsberg, they may at this very moment be tearing apart the monumental sets for Nina Petrovna's "wonderful lies" [i.e., *Die wunderbare Lüge der Nina Petrovna* (*The Wonderful Lies of Nina Petrovna*, 1929)] while we are busy shooting a few truths we consider important, for a laughably small sum of money.

*

In seeking the title, we spent a long time wavering between *Summer of '29* and *Young People Like Us*. To resolve this dilemma, we opted for *That's Exactly How Things Are*, because the title clearly states that what we're aiming for is less contrived and less busy, with less drama and less paper! The basis for the script is a reportage. In the course of one Saturday and one Sunday we followed five randomly selected young people and had a look at how they spent their weekend. The result was this film. A very, very simple story, quiet yet abounding in melodies that our ears pick up on every day. No stunts, no clever punch lines, even running the risk of having "not the foggiest notion of the laws of drama." The five people in this film, that's you and me. May God punish us, but our waiter is a good boy who lives in Neukölln and gambles away his 10 percent in cards; he is not like that former tsarist lieutenant, Smirnoff by name, who was impoverished by the course of events and also saved Anastasia's life. May God punish us, but our heroine types on a typewriter and does not have a pink divan on which she can coax the Przemisl fortification plans from the generals, deceptively masked spy that she actually is. Oh, yes, we lack a strong storyline, a tangible conflict, and God knows what else. Let's hope so. We skirted all the beaten paths for miles, on a narrow and utterly unused, terribly isolated route; the sign indicating the direction said "LIFE."

Rochus Gliese, who worked with Friedrich Wilhelm Murnau for many years, directed the film. Moriz Seeler, the eternal seeker and experimenter, kept all the pieces together. Robert Siodmak and Edgar Ulmer, two new names in Berlin, oversaw the camera work with Schüfftan, the cameraman; thank God they come neither from industry nor from literature. The five actors aren't actors either. For this documentary, we put together a cast of people from the same class, the same profession. Indeed, one character even plays himself. Plays? You have to have seen how the five young people move, how they look into the lens, how they blow their noses, and how they laugh: we wouldn't trade them for a dream cast . . .

Another four weeks. Without a studio or the funds available to the big studios, but with an idea that we deem worthwhile. At the end of the film we have a very short scene that may highlight everything most clearly: our fellows are standing in front of a movie theater in the suburbs after the Saturday and after the Sunday screenings by pure chance and without seeing it. Behind them, a poster shouts out: *Weekend Magic*. And that is the remoteness we want to show, between the weekend film inside and the Sunday that our five people have actually experienced.

Well, let's cross our fingers. For the sake of a good thing.

Tempo, July 23, 1929

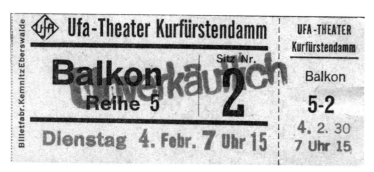

FIGURE 12. Ticket to the world premiere of *Menschen am Sonntag* on February 4, 1930.

How We Shot Our Studio Film

Billie Wilder wrote the screenplay for a film, People on Sunday, *which is being shown at the Ufa Theater on Kurfürstendamm. Here he reports how this film was created—without money, without a studio, without "experts," without any real organization. And how this film became a success anyway.*

We're sitting here and pinching ourselves. Eight times seven is fifty-six. Copenhagen is the capital of Denmark. No, we're not sleeping. So it's true. People are telling us: success. People are even telling us: great success. We are very happy.

We worked on our film for nine months. It was a rotten time. It was a lovely time.

"It's just going to work!"

A short fellow jumps up like a man possessed and pounds on the marble top. His glasses and the soda glasses quiver. Moriz Seeler.

We are five.

A Mr. Eugen Schüfftan, inventor of some sort of world-famous film trick that I fail to understand to this day, stares at him agape: "Without money?"

"Without money!"

The third man, Robert Siodmak, from Dresden (first news-paper, then theater, then film distribution) finds it hard not to burst out laughing: "Without a studio?"

"Without a studio!"

"Just like that?" Posing this question is Edgar Ulmer, twenty-three years old, emigrated from Hollywood half a year ago. Served as a set designer for Murnau's *Sunrise*.

"Just like that!"

I, Billie Wilder, am the fifth. "Then we're good to go?"

"Yes, indeed! Good to go. Just like that. Without a studio. Without money."

And that's how the film studio begins. At a coffeehouse table. In June 1929.

We do have a camera. That's all for now.

What do we want to shoot with it? A hundred ideas, a hun-dred suggestions. We get to the first slapstick scenes. We feel that we understand one another. And all of a sudden, the thing is right there: it has to be a very simple documentary film. A film about Berlin, about its people, about the everyday things we know so well. Our thoughts first turn to young actors. But the people have to be authentic. We look around. In front of a bar on Kurfürstendamm, Seeler comes across a chauffeur, taxi IA 10 068, Erwin Splettstösser. He signs on instantly. But Fräu-lein Borchert thinks we have something totally different in mind. She sells gramophone records. It takes a lot of effort to persuade her. Her family figures we're sex traffickers. In the end, though, she does agree to a screen test, at Thielplatz. Christl Ehlers comes, too; she already has experience, she once worked as an extra with E. A. Dupont and gives us her word of honor that she is on friendly footing with the recording manager of Lapa Pick. We bump into a von Waltershausen; he is exactly what we need.

Meanwhile, the screenplay is sketched out. Seven typed pages. We discover the trick: to concentrate Berlin into one Sunday.

But money, money! We have no film stock.

After a few weeks we get hold of a moneyman on Friedrichstrasse. We trick him with numbers. Three percent of his motivation was his belief in our abilities; 97 percent came from his interest in getting his hands on an incredibly cheap film. We draw up an insanely low cost estimate. Tell him about waltzes and a driver who is dying to get out. Eventually we land the deal; the contract is signed. The first thousand yards of film are issued to us. Things start up.

And boy, do they ever start up!

The five people we've chosen take vacation time. They get a flat rate from us, ten marks a day, and we compensate them for their loss of wages. Months, months. In the water, in the city. Every day someone else gives up, doesn't hold out. Insults turn to enthusiasm when we see the shots in the screening.

We are in the studio for a single day.

The weather gives us a hard time. We spend weeks waiting for a nice day. We're depressed. Will anything ever come of this? The "actors" grow impatient. The moneyman grows impatient and thinks his dough is down the drain.

Somehow or other we manage to finish.

No one still believes in it. On Friedrichstrasse they've heard something about it, now they're laughing at us. We sit there quietly and cut. We've used up ten thousand yards of film. God only knows where the money came from.

On December 11 the film is complete. We screen it for the men at one of the major film companies. We are not taken seriously. The head of the company tells us that after thirty years in the business he'd be willing to give up his job if this film ever somehow makes it as far as a showing, not to mention a

FIGURE 13. Poster for *Menschen am Sonntag*.

success. The "press officer" finds there is a lack of "psychological depth." We get this exact same reaction from three other companies.

A new financial backer has turned up. He may want to finance the nighttime performance for us. We screen the film at Ufa. Brodnitz, the director of the theater division, gets to see it. And takes it—for the regular evening program at U. T. Kurfürstendamm.

We are flabbergasted. The premiere is here.

When we take a bow at 9:00, we don't know what is going on. Are we being taken seriously, or are we being laughed at? In any case, between 9:00 and 9:13, with heart palpitations at their peak, we've thought of a topic for a new film.

Der Montag Morgen, February 10, 1930

Getting Books to Readers

A close acquaintance recently shot himself to death. He was a traveling book salesman. His collection, which he carried in a little cardboard suitcase, consisted of "thdee departbets," as he, condemned to a lifetime of sniffling, would say to his customers through his stuffed nose. These three departments were: on the left, "cribidal dovels," in the middle, "polidics," and on the right, "cdassics." Except for a battered volume of Peter Altenberg, missing pages 8 to 26, which he was never able to get rid of, his collection changed its look every few weeks. His business was going well. Suddenly we learn that he has shot himself to death—and that he did so out of desperation.

I cannot believe it. Recently I happen to have been spending a good deal of time in bookstores because I was interested in seeing people buy and sell books, but mainly to find out whether books are being bought at all. I watched carefully and sounded out the gentlemen there. Business is good. Of course, it has dropped a bit since Christmas. The important thing, however, is this: in Berlin, and, I may generalize, in Germany, many books are being bought at this very time. There is good reason for satisfaction.

So if my acquaintance has shot himself, it is unlikely that the cause was that no one is buying books. It is quite certain that hunger was not the reason he shot himself. But rather . . . we did all warn him about Amélie; we can't be held responsible.

•

One afternoon, in one of those splendid bookstores in the western part of Berlin that smells better than Coty and Chanel and features a charming disharmony of colorful book covers almost as pleasant to look at as women with ingeniously applied

makeup, one lady is there who is interested in American literature. She has a younger brother in Kansas, a pastor, and wants
to go see him. The salesman has to listen to this, has to lend his
ear to detailed family stories before finally pawning off a paperback edition of Egon Erwin Kisch's *Paradise America*.
A young married couple decides on a book by Siegfried von
Vegesack, *Love Non-Stop*. The two volumes of *The Battle for
Rome*, by the revered Felix Dahn, are being dusted off; a papa
takes them. A hopeful boy is likely to be celebrating his twelfth
birthday nearby tomorrow. A man who doesn't look the least
bit professorial still insists on the new *Propyläen History of
the World*, which carries the fresh scent of high-quality art
printing.

A conversation starts up with a gentleman who sells books
here. What takes off, what doesn't? What collects mildew on
the shelves, and what gets ripped out of your hands like rolls
right out of the oven? How do you give advice to a customer,
how do you get the customer to add on a second and third book?
And so forth.

*

Today's purchasers, particularly the superior ones, have a very
fine nose for good books, the gentleman behind the desk says.
Customers grow interested in publishing houses, which make
them think that the book must be high quality, aha, S. Fischer,
that won't be garbage! They gather advice from the newspaper
reviews. Every now and again they also take to heart endorsements by important contemporaries found on the books' jack-
ets, if these endorsements don't overtly smack of advertising.
They stop ignoring the displays and have nothing against getting catalogs of new publications sent to their homes.

The price of the book isn't the most important thing at all.
In France, people flock to cheap books even if they're printed

on paper so thick and hard that you can use a page from one of them to kill somebody. Or they're printed on toilet paper. They don't care. As long as it's cheap, cheap, cheap. Germans buy a book with the same seriousness used to buy something like a shirt. Durability is key. They have no intention of leaving the book on the train or throwing it into the corner like yesterday's newspaper. It has to have "lasting value." A piece of furniture. And a magnificent one at that. In Germany, they make far more tasteful books than, say, shirts. Just compare the display window of a bookstore with that of a shop selling woolens.

Trotsky's memoirs, Stefan Zweig's *Fouché*, Alfred Döblin's *Alexanderplatz* are the books of the day.

During my half-hour of observations, three copies of the Trotsky sell, one of *Fouché*, and a full four of Döblin's *Alexanderplatz*. The afternoon mail, which is just drifting in, brings letters with two more orders for Döblin's Berlin book, one from Munich and one from Riga. Memoirs, biographies are popular. Rudolf Olden's *Stresemann*, Hans von Seeck's *Future of the Empire*, René Fülöp-Miller's *Jesuits* are doing splendidly. Right behind Döblin in the category of novels is the new Leonhard Frank, *Brother and Sister*. Sarah Levy's *O mon Goye!* is also in high demand, surely in large part because of its cheeky title. In the historical documents, Theodor Pilvier's *The Kaiser's Coolies* and Werner Beumelburg's *Barrage around Germany* are off to an excellent start. The latest Jack London, *The Valley of the Moon*, can't complain, Hans Rudolf Berndorff's *Espionage* is approaching forty thousand copies sold.

There is some slight stagnation in crime stories. The success of extravagant mass productions has become quite iffy.

By contrast, illustrated animal books are selling wonderfully since Paul Eipper's *Animals Look at You!* Bengt Berg, for example. And the beautiful travel books. Günther Plüschow. Wilhelm Filchner.

That, in short, is the situation that can be surveyed on an afternoon in a Berlin bookstore.

But as far as "saddling" customers with a book, the gentlemen here will have no part of that. We don't force anything on the customers. Not us. We advise them. We shyly present books that might interest them. We let them leaf through the books as long as they like. We don't forget to point a customer who has bought some Erich Maria Remarque to Ludwig Renn, and to Georg Glaser. But we don't saddle them with anything. If the shop looks appealing they'll take something else with them, even if it's just a little paperback.

The methods of these gentlemen are clearly quite laudable.

In Texas, let's say, there may well be bookstores that don't operate in such a peaceful manner. As soon as a customer enters the shop, the door is locked from the inside, the seller puts the key into his pants pocket with a smile, and now the purchase begins. The poor man who has entered the shop to buy a timetable and was careless enough to leave his machine gun at home hardly stands a chance of getting back to the street alive without having purchased fifty books that he doesn't care a fig about or find interesting.

Try to imagine that on our end. That you're not let out of a bookstore until you buy a couple of books by Rudolph Stratz and a complete set of Rudolf Herzog. Thank you.

Der Querschnitt, issue 2, March 1930

How I Pumped Zaharoff for Money

I actually wanted to go to Heligoland, wanted to sit on the beach and play with shells. I ended up in Monte Carlo, sat in the casino, and played roulette. I had a burning desire to break the bank of Monte Carlo with my exceedingly surefire system.

Well—it didn't succeed in the slightest.

After ten days I was left high and dry. But what was even worse, when I wanted to go to bed one night, Hotel Savoy, room 37, I was not even allowed into the building. At the Riviera they have incredibly reliable X-ray vision, enabling them to see straight through the wallets of the unlucky gamblers. They hold off with the bill for three days, then they rattle off a few charming courtesies to guests and unceremoniously kick them out onto the street.

So that night I stood there, sleepy and freezing, my last ten francs in my tuxedo trousers.

I sat down on a bench at the promenade downstairs, counting all the palm trees; there were 127, I know the exact number. Then I spat into the Mediterranean another three times, which brought the number up to 130. Finally I prayed softly to the dear Lord that he would never, never again make the sun rise. After all, my tuxedo still made some sort of sense at night. But going around in a tuxedo during the day—that just isn't done. Distraught as I was, I ran up to Monaco, to the so-called suicide cliff, where so many longtime gamblers had put an end to their messed-up lives by taking a little leap into the abyss. On the way there it occurred to me that I knew a jazz player in the Café de Paris. I wanted to pump him for money. But he couldn't give me any. He did lend me an empty violin case, and that was already a big help. All of a sudden my tuxedo gained a reason for existence. For the following two days I ran back and forth like an unemployed violin virtuoso between Monte Carlo and Nice with an empty violin case under my arm and an empty stomach.

I dragged myself around like that for two days. I cleaned my tuxedo shirt with an eraser. Holes were already poking through the thin soles of my patent-leather shoes. I couldn't even think about what to do; my empty stomach utterly incapacitated me.

It was just awful. I was standing at the train station in Monte Carlo with my violin case, waiting for the express train from Marseille for no good reason. Maybe I subconsciously wanted to fling myself in front of the locomotive. I leafed through a German book that was on a sales display at the newspaper stand. The title was *How They Got Rich and Powerful*. Suddenly, I discovered in it the picture of an old man with a white goatee, in a high-necked gray overcoat and with a sort of pith helmet on his head. Under the picture it said: *Sir Basil Zaharoff.*

What made my knees tremble was the irrefutable fact that I knew this man by sight. So this man, whom I saw daily on my hunger marches, this man, whom I'd regarded as a fellow sufferer, was the richest man in Europe and the principal shareholder of the casino over there: so this man may be living off my twenty thousand francs at the moment, which I had placed on even instead of odd.

When the express train for Marseille arrived, I was already firmly resolved to pump him for money. I had to swindle him, preferably for a sum of four figures, in order not to starve, I swore to myself.

I knew for a fact that every morning between 8:30 and 9:30, Sir Basil Zaharoff took a stroll near the casino. He walked somewhat unsteadily, leaning on a cane, and after every ten steps he sat down on a bench to catch his breath.

My nerves were insanely tense as I sidled up to him the next morning. The sole of my right patent-leather shoe was no longer there, and I was already walking on my sock. My arm was so weak that the empty violin case felt like a truck. My breath grew fast and furious, my white lips trembled. Now I caught sight of him walking very slowly toward the bench I was standing at and quivering. His gray overcoat moved softly, his gray hat, which he wore like a pith helmet, sat so far down on his face that only the white goatee peeked out.

My God, the richest man in Europe. I had to hold on to the bench or I would have fallen onto the violin case with excitement.

Word of honor, we were sitting next to each other: Sir Basil Zaharoff, the billionaire, and me, the derelict without a centime to my name. I counted to twenty-five, mustered up my courage, and declared heroically, "Bonjour, Monsieur Zaharoff!" He peered over at me, looking quite unfriendly at first, but then he nodded. I spent a minute listening to my heart pounding, louder and louder. All of a sudden Zaharoff tapped my violin case with his walking stick and launched into a conversation about violin virtuosos: Fritz Kreisler, Bronisław Hubermann, and Jan Kubelik. My mind was racing, and I searched for a way of shifting the topic. I didn't find one, especially once Zaharoff remarked with some degree of pleasure that he thought it splendid that I played the violin and not roulette. Then he got up again and swayed over to the next bench. Rooted to the spot, I looked at him, incapable of running after him, falling to my knees before him, and declaring to him: "Monsieur, I'm starving!"

That afternoon, with the help of my empty violin case, I was able to get a booking as a jazz violinist in Venice. When it became evident that I did not have a violin, and could not even read a single note, I truly *had* been helped out by a friend.

Der Querschnitt, issue 3, March 1933

II

Portraits of Extraordinary and Ordinary People

Early on in his career as a journalist, Wilder demonstrated a re-markable talent for capturing the character of the cultural, ar-tistic, and political figures in his midst. While still in Vienna, he wrote evocative profiles of Danish actress Asta Nielsen, whose performances on the Austrian stage and screen were among the most celebrated of the era, and of the fabulously popular Tiller Girls, the British dance troupe that showed up at Vienna's West-bahnhof railway station in the spring of 1926. He also covered the Austrian jazz musician Toni Girardi and the momentous occasion when the American band leader Paul Whiteman graced Vienna with his presence; his profile of Whiteman, which noted the American jazzman's famous moustache, then dove beneath it to lay bare the whole man, led to a follow-up concert review from Berlin, lavishing further attention on Whiteman's outsize persona.

Wilder's portraits also include two separate pieces devoted to the Prince of Wales, a figure whose impressive sartorial hab-its and playboy demeanor held a certain fascination for young Billie (much later, he worked a passing reference to him into the dialogue for *The Front Page* [1974], one of his final movies), as well as his interview with American millionaire Cornelius Vanderbilt IV. Additional profiles include an account of the visit to Berlin by French writer Claude Anet (né Jean Schopfer), whose 1920 novel *Ariane, jeune fille russe* would serve as the source material for a script Wilder co-wrote with I. A. L. Diamond for *Love in the Afternoon* (1957); a sixtieth-birthday tribute to Felix Holländer, the German writer, critic, and frequent collaborator of theater impresario Max Reinhardt; and a tribute to his former mentor Klabund (Alfred Henschke) a year after Klabund's passing. Wilder's early love of film, and of the characters that inhabit that world, comes across vividly in his portraits of Erich von Stroheim ("The Man We Love to Hate") and of American actor Adolphe Menjou on tour in Berlin. Interspersed among the more famous profiles are chronicles of everyday lives, like an account of the oldest woman in Berlin, of a Swiss-born circus clown, of a *B. Z.* newspaper saleswoman, and of an uncommonly talented poker artist named Fritz Herrmann. Wilder's work on the script for *Menschen am Sonntag* took much the same direct, candid approach in representing everyday people with all their beauty, dignity, and truth.

Asta Nielsen's Theatrical Mission

AN INTERVIEW

The Raimund Theater is ablaze with light. The arc lamps are reflected in the wet asphalt, a long row of cars in front of the main entrance; the show must be ending soon. I have to hurry up if my plan is to succeed. I go in through the narrow stage door. The porter at the front desk is flipping through a newspaper. I try to sneak past him, but he's already caught sight of me. "What does the gentleman wish to do? This is not an entrance for outsiders!" I introduce myself and hold out my credentials for him to inspect. We negotiate for a full quarter of an hour. Then he leads me down a dim hallway and up to a door. "So, this is Frau Nielsen's dressing room. You have to wait. The show will be over in ten minutes." The porter slinks back to his desk; I wait and wait.

All of a sudden it occurs to me: how about I strike up a friendship with the coat-check girl in the meantime? As long as I get inside, even seven devils won't cast me out. I knock on the door. A booming man's voice answers, "Enterrr!"

A man? Did the porter show me to the wrong door? I turn the knob timidly, open the door halfway; a gentleman of medium height with an intelligent face, deep-set eyes, and a part in his hair comes toward me; at one point I must have seen him somewhere. "Yes?" "Pardon me, Sir, if I'm disturbing you. The porter showed me to this door. . . . I'm a journalist. . . . And people are interested in Asta Nielsen's path from the movies to the stage. So I wanted to do a little interview, with the artist herself . . ." "Is that so? Well, then, that's fine. Perhaps you can take a seat here. My wife will be coming soon. And please allow me to introduce myself: Gregori Chmara is my name."

Now I know where I know him from: he is the same Chmara who acted under Konstantin Stanislavski in Vienna, has been making films in Germany for several years, and just recently became Asta Nielsen's husband. He is adept at chatting, still struggling with the language, searching for words.

"Yes, it was my idea for Asta to take to the stage. I grew up in the theater; acted with Stanislavski for years. In 1922 I was in Berlin; it was there that I saw Nielsen for the first time. Now we're married. As long as film gave us projects in which we flourished, we didn't think about the theater. But today, when American kitsch has killed off the German art film? Is Asta Nielsen supposed to stand still on the same dead spot? And so it came that Nielsen turned her back on the camera and headed to the stage, as I always wanted."—"And you, Herr Chmara? Will you also act in the theater in Germany?" "I hope so! But it can take years for me to gain a good command of the language. In the meantime, I'm going over my wife's roles with her, helping her, working as her director and—if you will—her impresario."

Now there's noise from the cloakroom. Steps. Voices. The show seems to be over. A few more minutes and the door opens: Asta Nielsen steps quickly into the room. Tall, slender, black-haired. Three things stand out to me: her big brown eyes, always tear-filled; her jet-black tresses, smoothed back; her snow-white, long, unnerving hands. Just three weeks ago I saw her in a movie—it was called *Frau im Feuer* (*The Woman in Flames*, 1924) or something like that—and now she is standing in front of me, quite close, so close that I feel her warm breath. Chmara introduces us. Asta is tired, it's easy to see. But Asta is nice; she sits down at the table like a schoolgirl as Chmara's hand strokes her hair. (The two of them love each other like seventeen-year-olds.) I keep it brief. Asta Nielsen gives her responses quickly and concisely. She speaks with a foreign accent, somewhat like a Brit, but fluently and easy to understand. "So you've left movies for good?"

"No, I've left them because they didn't have any new real projects for me. But I will belong to them once again when they become art. For me, film and theater are one and the same. I've stayed true to myself." "You already acted in the theater?" "Yes, indeed: for nine years in my hometown of Copenhagen. Then I went into motion pictures. Waldemar Psilander was my first partner. I spent fifteen years in front of the camera."

"How do you feel as a newborn theater actress?" "I'm happy. I owe a great deal to my husband, who has made me into a Stanislavski actress." "The play?" "Sheldon's *Romance*. A cleverly constructed drama that ran for three years in America. My role? An Italian singer who has to speak with a foreign accent." "Your next plans, your next roles?" "I'm traveling to Berlin. Negotiations with a particular theater are being concluded. I'll be acting in August Strindberg's *Rausch* (*Intoxication*). Maybe *Hamlet*, too." "Why don't you go to America?" "Oh—I would never have been happy in America! There's no sense of culture there, no art." "Whom do you regard as the best film actor?" "Everyone has his roles. These actors have made the greatest impression on me: Werner Krauss in *Caligari* (1920); Emil Jannings in *Varieté* (*Variety*, 1925); Gregori Chmara in *Raskolnikow* (*Crime and Punishment*, 1925); a highly creative genius is Charlie Chaplin; I think Lon Chaney is overrated." "Your best film?" "*Fräulein Julie* (*Miss Julie*, 1922)!" "What do you do, Madam, when you aren't doing anything?" "I talk to my husband about the theater. It's lucky that I can talk things out with him. Or else I sleep."—"How long have you been wearing your hair in a bob?" "For five years. I had my hair cut for the Hamlet film." "What does a man need to look like for you to find him attractive?" "Like Chmara." "Are you for or against the British mustache?" "I must confess: an idea that deep has never weighed on my mind." "One more stupid question . . ." "Cross that out!"

Asta Nielsen, the world's greatest film actress, will not be on the screen for a long time. The many thousands of people who were able to admire her brilliant art will shrink down to hundreds. And that, I think, is a misfortune.

Die Bühne, February 4, 1926

My "Prince of Wales"

I actually wanted to interview the Prince of Wales. A few nice lines about British fashion are always of interest. Yes, but where, how, when? A couple of days ago a New York newspaper ran a picture of the prince, perched on a little ledge in the middle of a diabolical waterfall, a fishing rod with the gold handle between his legs, puffing on his pipe and grinning: "His Majesty the British son of the king, fishing in Dalmellington, Scotland."

In Scotland! One thousand fifty miles from the Opernring in Vienna, as the crow flies. So what do I do? Go there? Interview him by telegraph? Wait till he comes to Vienna. Or how about this—

There must be an Englishman in Vienna who knows about fashion. If not the king of fashion himself, at least someone from his kingdom. And where do I find him? Child's play! In the hotels, of course. In front of the Imperial, I find confirmation for my shrewd deductions. Someone is standing there: lean, manly, in seriously casual clothing, inherently elegant, distinguished, Oxford trousers, short, double-breasted overcoat, his hat pushed down deep onto his face, in his right hand a walking stick as thick as a tree trunk. A Brit, by God, a typical Brit! So off I go! (There must be impertinent journalists in England as well.) "Excuse me . . ."

The Englishman is a nice, amiable gentleman (just as we learned in school). Five minutes later, when we are sitting in a corner at a coffeehouse, I already know everything: he is originally from Cardiff, studied at Cambridge, is now here from Italy, enjoying central Europe on the way back, charmed by Vienna, speaks good German, spits expertly, makes his pipe saunter from one corner of his mouth to the other, elegantly and in a flash, and knows a great deal about fashion, which is the main thing as far as I'm concerned.

"The latest fashion? The very same as we've had for ten, twenty, and thirty years, the same as we'll have in a hundred years." That is indeed the major difference between British and French, American, and Italian fashion. An Englishman orders ten suits and five pairs of shoes at a time. At a time! He changes his clothes daily, always looks elegant, and is not bothered by shoemakers and tailors for five years. An American buys himself a new suit every summer, every winter, wears it day after day, then tosses it into the trash can after six months. He does the same with his hats and everything else! He follows fashion, to the extent that this can be called fashion. Today his jacket needs to have four buttons, his overcoat needs a velvet collar, his shoes need to be wing-tipped; tomorrow he will put a green band on his straw hat, and his waist needs to "fall" exactly three inches above his appendix. Business, nothing but business! The same applies to French, Italian, or any fashion. Practical, unobtrusive, elegant: that is the inclination of the well-dressed Englishman.

His clothes have to be of the best fabric, his shoes of the finest leather, his shirts of pure silk. Anything that is expensive is good, anything that is good lasts a long time, and anything that lasts a long time is not expensive enough! "The suit you see here"—he points to his dark gray sports jacket, to his flannel trousers, all perfectly new, as if straight from the shop window, a fabulous fit, "this suit is three and a half years old! I had it made in London at the top tailor's for twenty-two pounds. I'm the picture of foolishness, you're thinking? Add it up! Three and a half years and counting. An American needs seven suits for this period of time. And I hope to be able to wear mine for another good three years. You're amazed? Just a moment! How old do your ties normally get?" The Englishman glances sympathetically at my tie, the little knot of which sits impeccably on the stiff collar. "Half a year at most."

"Half a year? Do you know how long I've been wearing my ties? Three and four years! Yes, indeed! But have a look at the quality, and take a look at the way it's tied: the knot is big, tied casually. Being creased on a daily basis ruins even the best tie. And what good is a stiff collar? Washing it is expensive, and your neck gets chafed and painful. We wear it only with a tuxedo and tails. Otherwise just soft collars. You see, the structure leaves a bit of space free for the knot here, which means that the collar will always fit even it's too small or too large." "And doesn't fashion ever offer anything new?"

"New? Nothing but minor details. Ultimately it makes no difference whether the trousers are an inch and a half longer, the lapels three-fourths of an inch wider. The suit always has a casual cut, with long, wide Oxford trousers and unwaisted short jacket. The overcoat, also unwaisted, is long. Here it's rare to see the all-weather coat that is so popular there. It serves as a raincoat, a winter coat, and a coat for between seasons. Hats are light, made of the best felt. Shoes are always rounded, rough leather, and thick-soled. Patent-leather shoes without toe caps. Wearing undershirts goes a long way toward minimizing wear and tear on shirts. Why undershirts? Practical, my dearest, practical, nothing but practical. There's nothing else to say about us. You must already be aware that we always puff on pipes, spit with passion, play soccer devotedly, and are blessed with hearing like a congested walrus!"

A clever fellow, this Englishman! By the way, he's brought me around to this taste in clothing: I'm going to dress in the English way, starting today! Because going English is cheap, and what is cheap enough these days?

Die Bühne, February 11, 1926

Lubitsch Discovers

A CASTING BY AMERICA'S GREAT DIRECTOR

Daisy is determined to enter the world of film. She signs up for an appointment with Lubitsch and waits out the three days until she can finally go into the room of the Almighty One.

"What can I do for you?"

"I want to be in films!"

"Show me your feet!"

Daisy awkwardly lifts up her skirt until just above the knee.

"Not bad! Your other foot, please!"

Daisy bashfully replies, "It looks just like the other one!"

"Is that right? You're hired. For my next film: *The Lady with the Two Left Feet!*"

Die Bühne, February 18, 1926

FIGURE 14. "Die Tiller Girls sind da!" announces the arrival of the Tiller Girls in Vienna, *Die Stunde* (April 3, 1926).

The Tiller Girls Are Here!

THEY ARRIVED THIS MORNING AT THE WESTBAHNHOF

This morning, thirty-four of the most enticing legs emerged from the Berlin express train when it arrived at the Westbahnhof station. The charming ladies to whom they belonged had stylish traveling outfits on, and one of the last to leave the sleeping car was a tall, elegant lady of a certain age, an old-fashioned hat atop her somewhat flattened head, a lorgnette in her right hand, whirling her left hand in the air in the style of a musical conductor.

Someone wanted to know: "A girls' boarding school, certainly."

"Haha! April 2!"

These are the Tiller Girls, the charming Lawrence Tiller Girls from Manchester. Everyone is chirpy, busily squealing and giggling. You don't know where to look first. Sixteen magnificent girls, gathered together, cultivated in all parts of the world. Those figures, those legs, those little faces, and well bred to boot; aristocratic, you might say.

Miss Harley—such is the name of the shepherdess of these little sheep—is directing the operations, and everything works perfectly: the suitcases, the passports, everything is fine. The girls stand at attention in rank and file, awaiting Miss Harley's sharp commands. All around is the reception committee of curiosity seekers.

An interview will have to be conducted. Sixteen girls— sixteen questions. And off we go.

Blonde Winnie is up first. "Have you ever been in Vienna before?" "Vienna? No, but the Prater is supposed to be very beautiful."

Maisie, the left wingman, is the tallest. "You speak only English?" "*Nein. Ich sprechen auch deutsch: Ich liebe dich.*" (Terrible. I would have liked to ask her another question.)

Lilian, the shortest, has coal-black eyes. "Do you dance the Charleston?" "Yes, we dance the Charleston in the show."

Mabel, the prettiest one, seems not to be the brainiest. "What do you think of Einstein's theory of relativity?" "Einstein, Einstein . . . oh, *das sein* a good candymaker in Berlin."

Dorothy has lovely eyelashes, and knows how to flirt. "Which boarding school were you educated at?" "At the Convent of the Holy Virgin."

Marjorie, the one with the impish face, is the smartest. She also speaks the best German, and in Berlin she gave an address to the German press. "Do you consider Geneva pointless?" "Definitely. Politics ruins your character, and I want to hold onto mine."

Hilda I has big sweet round eyes. "Do you dance the waltz?" "With great pleasure. In Vienna I want to dance only the waltz. By Strauss."

Esther has a dreamy look about her. "Who is your ideal man? Stresemann, Jannings, or Dempsey?" "Rudolph Valentino."

Vera has a very delicate little face. "Are you for bobbed hair or the Eton crop?" "Always bobbed hair."

Hilda II always tilts her head. "Do you believe in love at first sight?" "When I look at you, *yes*."

Molly is a little chubby but has a nice laugh. "How do you picture your future?" "I will marry, definitely."

Olive has splendid teeth. "What do you think of short skirts?" "If you have pretty legs, like Flossie, Vera, Molly, Marjorie, Mabel, and Maisie, then the shorter, the better."

Joyce laughs seductively. "Bernard Shaw?" "I don't know, don't know him."

Flossie is serious. "Do you know Hamlet?" "Yes. A good play. Why doesn't this Shakespeare write any shows?"

Jessie is always upbeat. "Are you really watched over so strictly?" "Psst . . ." and places her index finger on her rosy little mouth.

Edith, elegant and well groomed, is the last. "What do you think of Austria and Slovakia getting closer?" "*Das Bester.*"

Miss Harley also gets a question. "Who is Tiller?" "John and Lawrence Tiller are the founders of the world-famous Girl University. At the age of ten the applicants with the best figures are accepted after passing an extensive test, then study for seven years. That is difficult work. Dance groups consisting of the best pupils are put together after the 'Matura' diploma: The Tiller Girls. The group I'm leading is one of the forty-seven who now perform around the world. A sound enterprise, respectable and world-renowned."

And Miss Harley again holds her lorgnette in front of her mouse-gray eyes, giving orders. The girls are brought home like a cash transport, hidden from public view.

They live in the Hotel . . .

But the only contact with them is at the Haller revue.

Die Stunde, April 3, 1926

The Tiller Girls' Boarding School at the Prater

The sixteen girls who paid a visit to the Prater in Vienna on a sunny spring day about a week ago—stylish, English-speaking, and walking two by two—were regarded by most of the passersby as the schoolchildren of a prestigious boarding school, particularly because an older woman was guarding them and ordering them about at every turn. But the fact that this girls' excursion included some young men and a photographer whose right hand carried a tripod and whose round back hauled a massive camera, not to mention the striking snazziness of all these girls, had to indicate to any viewer, assuming he was halfway intelligent and had studied the newspapers of the past few days and was able to tell the difference between English and Serbian, that these were the Tiller Girls.

On the first day of their stay in Vienna, these wonderful girls discovered the Apollo Theater; on the second day, St. Stephen's Tower, the bar at the Sacher Hotel, and the Diana Spa; and on the third, they headed off to the Prater; a little ride on a scenic railway, a little Viennese coffee—*the best in the world*—a little "merry-go-round": *awful nice!*

A Tiller Girl is pretty, stylish, pleasant, reasonably well educated, graceful, quick-witted, tactful, diplomatic, sweet; a Tiller Girl is all of that. Each one: Esther, Marjorie, Hilda I, Hilda II, Dorothy, Mabel, Lilian, Winnie, Maisie, Vera, Molly, Olive, Joyce, Flossie, Jessie, and Edith.

They all have the same taste, all hold the same opinion. They are one single entity, one single organism, all relying on the others. No individuality here. The absolute democracy.

"Mightn't, say, the Hoffmann Girls be better?"

A single cry of indignation makes the rounds, from Tiller Girl to Tiller Girl. Then there's a chorus: Tiller Girls—often copied, never equaled.

They rode on the roller coaster four times, and found that quite a bit of fun. They were also delighted with the Ferris wheel: Vienna . . . ! They stayed at the bumper car arena for a fun-filled half-hour. Each of them ate three portions of ice cream in some little confectionery. They shot at eggshells dancing on a water jet. They took so much pleasure in everything. But, being Englishwomen, they didn't want to ride the chariots with little donkeys harnessed to them, nor did they want to ride on the carousel with the chamber pots; they're ladies.

The littlest things captured their interest: they had to be everywhere. For Director Alexander from the Apollo and the charming Fritz Jacobsohn from Haller, this was serious business. And they always had to give in. How could they possibly resist entreaties from sweet Marjorie? Or a friendly kiss from Winnie?

Delightful people. Excursions should only be made with Tiller Girls. Perhaps it is the allure of the foreign language, perhaps the spontaneity of the girls, who are only kids. Great fun is had. One of the Hildas has hidden Jacobsohn's hat. Jessie is about to tuck a colorful piece of paper under Director Alexander's jacket collar, Mabel chats with the photographer about the beauty of the Scottish landscape, Dorothy and Olive quarrel, Molly holds Miss Harley, the leader, by her arm and guides her from booth to booth.

They like it here. The amusement park is larger, but the Prater is jollier. London is colossal, Berlin spectacular; but in Vienna there are such good schnitzels, such wonderful sweets. They would so like to stay on in Vienna. But on the first of the month they have to go to Dresden, then to Hamburg, and back to Berlin.

We discovered all that in a Prater snack bar. The girls are all forthright; they even own up to having a "darling" when that is the case. And Miss Harley, the governess, is allowed to hear it.

Let's stay indiscreet: you even get a (harmless, unerotic, friendly, cousinly, for God's sake obligation-free, forgotten the next minute . . .) little kiss, if you beg for one. God knows that's no simple matter. But you get it.

Say it came from Billie.

Die Bühne, April 15, 1926

Girardi's Son Plays Jazz at the Mary Bar

While his father is celebrating his professional milestone and posters on the streets request donations for a monument to this most popular person in Vienna—along with Mayor Karl Lueger—while a theater acts out the story of his life every evening and an exhibit dedicated to Girardi shows his realia to the Viennese, Toni plays jazz at the Mary Bar.

Toni Girardi is just twenty-eight years old, and people even claim to see a certain—outer—resemblance to his great father. He sits there, in front of the big drum, the drumsticks in his hands, works with all the instruments, the triangle, the cymbals, various whistles, and comically constructed thingamajigs that produce all sorts of exotic noise. Toni works with all of it, full of enthusiasm and love for the profession. Sometimes he even sings, when there's a jolly atmosphere. "*I love Ukulele Lady, Ukulele . . .*" Oh, Toni is a good jazz band player.

"So, you've become a jazz band player? Very interesting. If father only . . ."

"Oh, fiddlesticks. You have to make a living. Minimum wages at Jarno . . ." "You've been through quite a lot?" "Oh, yeah. The old man didn't want me to become an actor. No doubt he himself had a rotten time with this profession. But then he did sign my first contract for St. Pölten. Then I got married and went to work for my father-in-law in the car business. I liked that. Then I got divorced and remarried. Oh, well. At Jarno I acted again. I'm supposed to live on minimum wage. Two million."

During this conversation Toni goes on playing, warbling the melody to himself: "*. . . ein Gra-, ein Grammophon . . . Küss' die Hand, gnä Frau . . . das macht so schön trara, trara, Sie wissen schon . . .*"

"I had no more desire to keep on acting and wanted to go back to the car business. Easier said than done. Then I announced that I wanted to become a chauffeur. No reaction from anyone. Now I play jazz over there in the bar. You have to make a living."

And once again, the drumsticks in Toni's hands start to whirl.

Die Stunde, May 22, 1926

Paul Whiteman, His Mustache, the Cobenzl, and the Taverns

AN AFTERNOON WITH AMERICA'S SECOND MOST FAMOUS MAN

1.

In January of this year, the *Chicago Tribune* published statistics about the top-rated American celebrities. Millions cast their votes; the entire U.S. was in a flurry of excitement.

The statistics went like this: 1. Charlie Chaplin; 2. Paul Whiteman; 3. Jack Dempsey; 4. Ford; 5. Douglas Fairbanks; 6. Edison; 7. Johnny Weissmuller; 8. Rudolph Valentino; 9. Lillian Gish; 10. Rockefeller; 11. Tilden; 12. Coolidge.

Voice of the people—voice of God.

2.

Yesterday at noon, number 2 on the above-mentioned statistical list got out of a sleeping car of the express train from Berlin to Vienna.

If you add these things together—the most amusing mustache you could imagine, a truly charming little double chin, two gentle, childlike eyes in a nice broad face, a burly, graceful, tall man, dressed casually and unobtrusively—you get Paul Whiteman.

He is accompanied by Fritz Wreede, the well-known Berlin publisher, Paul's personal friend—his publisher, not his manager, as is being erroneously reported.

The "welcoming committee"—the two directors of the Wiener Boheme Verlag, Otto and Erwin Hem, composer Dr. Robert Katscher, Herr Armin Robinson, the Berlin managing director of the Boheme Verlag, a dozen enthusiasts, several journalists—are quickly introduced, a six-man band plays Whiteman's big American hit song, "Wonderful One . . . ," Whiteman happily shakes the conductor's hand, two photographers capture his portrait, and the whole group gets into the three cars waiting outside. Paul Whiteman, America's second most famous man, rides down Porzellangasse.

3.

He's staying at the old Hotel Bristol. In the bar downstairs, while the new arrivals are enjoying beer and sandwiches, there's time to put Whiteman under a magnifying glass and examine him in slow motion.

There's that mustache of his again, a splendid, peerless, divine, superb mustache. It alone would have made Paul famous, without a doubt. It is cut quite short and twirled up in the middle, the two ends extend out quite far, and it points upward toward his nostrils at a sharp angle; the tips have a bit of pomade, which adds an aromatic element to our visual pleasure. That is the mustache of the future. Copyright by Paul Whiteman.

Whiteman is drinking beer, Schwechater lager, and he likes the taste. "Wonderful," he says, and lifts his upper lip in ecstasy, which makes the ends of his mustache tickle his nose; that is Paul's way of displaying his enthusiasm. He doesn't speak a single word of German, even though his forefathers were Germans, his youth, his career, etc. . . . all of that is already well known. It's important to come up with very different kinds of questions.

"In your opinion, what influence does the prohibition of alcohol in America have on music?"

"*It is killing everything!*" comes the reply, in English. And Paul takes such a big swig out of his beer stein that the foam sticks to his mustache. The messenger boys come running: Theater a. d. Wien is on the telephone, Max Reinhardt is on the line, Herr Kalman is there with his car, Franz Lehar announces his arrival. . . . Fritz Wreede isn't having an easy time of it, his friend's fame is making things tough on him. Meanwhile, Paul Whiteman stays quiet, like a child prodigy who doesn't know what to make of everything while the eyes of the world are upon him.

"So you'll be performing in Vienna?"

"I'd be delighted to. But first I have three concerts in Holland, then I'll perform in Berlin, then in Paris. In late June I could do something in Vienna. But everything's still up in the air."

"Do you yourself play?"

"No, not anymore. I now conduct. With my knee."

"–?–?"

"Yes, with my knee."

The mustache flies up onto the left half of his face; my gullibility amuses him. "Look, like this!" Whitman got up and shook his right leg as though it had just fallen asleep and he wanted to wake it up.

"Sometimes my band even plays in the dark. The tango, for example. Then I conduct with a flashlight."

"What are your latest hits?"

"*How* and *Dreaming of a Castle in the Air*, and George Gershwin's *Rhapsody in Blue*."

"Will you be playing Viennese composers?"

"Yes, *Madonna*, by Robert Katscher; *Im Ural*, by Mr. Ralph Erwin; *Catharine*, by Fall, was a big hit with us. *Uonderfuhl*!"

4.

In the afternoon, Whiteman is shown a miniature version of Vienna, a tour of the Ring, the Cobenzl Castle, and the taverns.

Fritz Wreede introduces the city hall to him as Vienna's central kiosk, the Burgtheater as a swimming pool, and the university as our equestrian school. Not a single muscle twitches on Whiteman's face; he doesn't care. Dr. Katscher's supercharged Mercedes flies up the winding Cobenzl road—if the street weren't tarred, there would have been a big trail of dust. And the motor sings, "Mercedes, you are faster than the sunshine." Still, Paul Whiteman is unimpressed; he is used to his $18,000, 120-horsepower car.

Upstairs, however, the view begins to bring some hint of emotion to his mustache.

We drink a quart of "Spezial" at Manhart's. Whiteman seems to know something about wine: we'll stay with this one! The tavern singers perform our special songs for Whiteman: "*Mei muatterl war a echt's Weana-Kind*" (My Mama Was a True Child of Old Vienna) and "*Im Prater blühen wieder die Bäume*" (The Trees Are In Bloom Again in the Prater). "*Uonderfuhl*," he says, for he is polite.

Die Stunde, June 13, 1926

Whiteman Triumphs in Berlin

AUDIENCE OF FOUR THOUSAND AT THE PREMIERE IN THE GROSSES SCHAUSPIELHAUS

Special report in *Die Stunde*

Berlin, June 27, 1926

The concert begins on Saturday evening at 8:15. Berlin, musical and artistic Berlin, is in a state of feverish excitement. The Grosses Schauspielhaus is sold out, right down to the last seat. Paul Whiteman, Dr. Robert Katscher, and I head off to it. The clock on Potsdamer Platz reads ten minutes after eight. The cars are backed up all the way to Brandenburger Tor, and at Schiffbauer Damm the traffic moves only in fits and starts. There are eight hundred cars standing there. All of Berlin has gathered together; Berlin is dressed to the nines. We have to get out a hundred steps before the theater or it would take too long. The people have recognized Whiteman; after all, his picture is hanging on all the advertising pillars.

People are cheering for him before they've heard even one sound.

Three thousand five hundred people go into the Schauspielhaus, and four thousand are inside. Folding chairs are set up; two armchairs seat three. Eight to ten people are standing in the box section.

About five hundred have finagled their way in. Out on the street, cars continue to drive up. People are already offering 200 marks (that is, 340 schillings) for a single ticket. The luminaries include Prince Joachim of Prussia; officials from the American, French, and British embassies; the editor in chief of the *Berliner Tageblatt*, Theodor Wolf; the editor in chief of the *Vossische*

Zeitung, Georg Bernhard; the top music critics from all the Berlin papers; the directors of the Berlin Theater that are currently in Berlin; Emil Jannings and his wife; Fritz Kreisler and his wife; all the musicians available in Berlin, etc., etc. At 8:45, twenty-nine stylish Americans, all in tuxes, take to the podium and get to work on their instruments. Sudden silence. Whiteman gracefully prances onto the stage. Applause. Whiteman thanks the audience with a grin, his little mustache twitching, then he reaches for the baton. The room grows dark, a violet spotlight casting ambient light over the orchestra.

A call for quiet comes. It's beginning.

The first piece is "Mississippi." Naturalistic music. We hear the burble of water while experiencing the fabulous Mardi Gras celebrations in the river city of New Orleans. A musical piece of great interest.

Then come five American melodies. Whiteman is now conducting without a baton. His body vibrates, his double chin shudders, his mustache leaps, his knees quiver. Rhythm personified ("Tiger"), a ragtime piece ("Dizzy Fingers"), a frenetic chase across the scales ("Caprice Viennoise"), Kreisler's violin opus transformed into jazz. The thirty men are extraordinary musicians and extraordinary actors. Right in the middle of performing a musical number, they launch into a delightful comedy. The saxophone player flirts with a lady in a box seat while Whiteman looks daggers at him. The drummer falls asleep, the banjo player holds monologues. A musical joke is orchestrated.

The concert hall grows so dark that people can't see their programs. Whiteman keeps his boys in line with a flashlight, one after another. They are—all for one and one for all—first-class acts in a first-class music hall. As the violinist plays, he twirls his fiddle in the air, scratches his neck with the bow, then clamps it between his knees and fiddles away on the violin in this position. One of them plays on a simple tire pump; three men sing "Castles in the Air."

Suddenly the beam of light from Whiteman's flashlight lands on a corner where the musicians who are idle at the moment are drinking alcohol. The bottle is hidden, a guilty-looking musician scrambles to put on his most innocent face as though it were not he doing the drinking, but the cello. Brilliant comedians, brilliant musicians. The piano virtuoso is a sensation in his own right. His name is Perella, and once he goes up onto the concert stage alone, his name will have a marvelous ring to it. Katscher's "Madonna" and Josef Padilla's "Valencia," both arranged by Whiteman, are received enthusiastically. The audience goes crazy, and "Madonna," which is superbly orchestrated, can barely be recognized. It starts like a barcarole and ends with a Charleston that sets your legs atwitter. The "Rhapsody in Blue," a composition that created quite a stir over in the States, is an experiment in exploiting the rhythms of American folk music. When Whiteman plays it, it is a great piece of artistry. He has to do encores again and again. The normally standoffish people of Berlin are singing his praises. People stay on in the theater half an hour after the concert.

For jazz? Against jazz? The most modern of all music? Kitsch? Art?

Necessity! An essential regeneration of Europe's calcified blood.

Die Stunde, June 29, 1926

I Interview Mr. Vanderbilt

A CONVERSATION WITH THE AMERICAN
MULTIMILLIONAIRE——HE CARRIES ONLY
250 MARKS WITH HIM——HE ALSO HAS NO
TIME TO GO TO THE DENTIST

Berlin, July 7 [1926]

"That's him!"

The concierge raises his hand in excitement, the small bluish veins at his temples bulging. The director fiddles self-consciously with his tie. Twenty bellhops stand at attention.

The man causing this excitement is standing nonchalantly in the hall, gangling, about thirty, not especially elegant, his eyes mouse-gray and hard, his chin assertive. He exemplifies the young American businessman.

The whole hotel is fascinated by the name, dumbfounded and stunned.

Meanwhile, the bearer of this name shakes my hand cordially.

"An interview? All right!" And graciously invites me into the elevator, which the elevator boy—trembling, with beads of sweat on his forehead—directs to the third floor.

*

The man sitting across from me is a Vanderbilt, a member of the American billionaire family; he's so rich that if the urge should strike, he could buy the entire Unter den Linden including the Brandenburger Tor, just for fun.

"I am Cornelius Vanderbilt Jr.," he says, full of kindness and warmth. While speaking he displays a sturdy but flawed set of teeth. *Why doesn't he go to the dentist?* the interviewer wonders.

He finally gets the answer half an hour later: Mr. Vanderbilt has no time for dentists; he has to work, work hard and always.

"The father of my great-grandfather made our fortune, made our name. He was Dutch and settled in America when New York was still New Amsterdam. I am the only male descendant of the fifth generation of the Vanderbilts."

He states this rather simply and without a trace of pathos, as though he were anyone but the heir to hundreds of millions of dollars.

"You will excuse me if I now tidy up a bit."

Of course I will excuse him.

Mr. Vanderbilt takes off his coat and trousers and changes his shoes.

I find out:

Mr. Vanderbilt's shoes have new soles;

Mr. Vanderbilt's trousers are a bit frayed;

Mr. Vanderbilt's overcoat is shiny at the elbows;

Mr. Vanderbilt's tie has a grease stain.

*

"Wonderful thing to be a journalist. When I was twenty-two I started as a newspaper reporter at the *New York Herald* and the *New York Times*. Today I'm twenty-eight; I'm the owner of three newspapers: two in California, one in Miami, Florida. Additionally, I have two magazines and a publication company that extends across the entire U.S. and employs eight thousand workers. I always live in New York. Would you like to visit me sometime? Here is my address."

His slender hand extends a card to me:

Mr. CORNELIUS VANDERBILT, JR.

New York, 640 Fifth Avenue

"You'd also like to know what I'm doing in Europe? A little educational trip. I write political portraits of European statesmen for my papers. Last week I spoke with Mussolini, yesterday with Piłsudski. I'm all wrapped up in my profession. As I said: Wonderful thing to be a journalist."

Mr. Vanderbilt's eyes light up when he talks about the term "newspaper." An enthusiast.

*

Couriers come running, the telephone rings off the hook. Berlin is looking for Mr. Vanderbilt. "I need to keep it brief. Ten questions. No more."

"Yes."

"First: What would you do if you were a poor European?"

"I would become a newspaper man. Unquestionably and definitely."

"Second: Do you consider it possible to save the French franc without American help?"

"I can't say. I'm a politician, not a financier."

"Third: Your favorite sport?"

"Sailing."

"Fourth: How much money do you usually carry with you?"

"Not much." He digs into his pocket and pulls out a wad of cash. Two hundred fifty marks, all told, not one penny more. "But I also have a checkbook with me!" That is a thing of beauty, this oblong little checkbook, bound in patent leather. "How many zeroes can be put on it?" "You're good for the money!" "I hope so," he replies in English.

"Fifth: your impressions of Berlin as a big city?"

"I know Berlin, was already here in 1912. I like the city much better now. Gotten big. Its traffic comes up to our standards. I love the greenery in Berlin, its gardens and parks. Truly."

"Sixth: Whom do you consider the more important comedian, Charlie Chaplin or Buster Keaton?"

"Charlie Chaplin."

"Seventh: how many begging letters do you get in a day?"

"Six hundred."

"Eighth: Do you find that wealth makes people arrogant?"

"Hmm. I have so much work to do that I don't get around to thinking about whether being rich makes me happy or bored."

"Ninth: what feeling do you get when you see an interviewer?"

"A wonderful, delightful feeling of happiness comes over me. From the standpoint of the businessman, of course. My friend Ford got rich on the strength of interviews and anecdotes. You have to be interviewed a hundred times, you have to take pride in the knowledge that your cars are being compared to canned food in so and so many jokes. Business, my dear man, business . . ."

"Tenth: do you identify as a billionaire or as a journalist?"

"Journalist!"

"Well, then, goodbye, *Herr Kollege*."

Mister Vanderbilt laughs so heartily that his bad teeth can be seen once again. But now I know for sure: he truly has no time to visit a dentist.

Die Stunde, July 10, 1926

The Prince of Wales Goes on Holiday

What is the Prince of Wales? *A funny boy*, a snazzy guy.

And how is life at the court? He's sick and tired of it.

How Buckingham Palace bores him! And Windsor Castle. And his Marlborough House. And the Osborne House summer residence on the Isle of Wight. And Balmoral in Scotland.

So how is *the world's most popular young man* feeling? Bored stiff and deeply unhappy.

It doesn't even pay to run incognito to the London bars, to the Kit-Kat Club, where they've been playing the same songs for seven weeks, "Baby Face" and "Charlie My Boy," "Charlie My Boy" and "Baby Face."

Yes, and those fellows on Sandringham in Norfolk play golf so badly that the chickens get a good laugh.

There's still the greyhound races in White City; it is a fine thing, once, twice, then even the electric hare makes you yawn.

There's still a little outing with the royal yacht, oh, very pleasant if you weren't disturbed every moment by cross-Channel swimmers and the whirring of flights over the ocean.

There might still be a cute little tumble from a horse, in the presence of members of the press and their photographers. But that is an old repertoire; his majesty the prince has indulged in a bit of a slip off the horse—one little tumble per season—back in 1926, 1925, 1924, 1923, 1922 . . .

A world that—God have mercy. So dull, sooo dull.

Another trip around the world?

Hmm, hmm.

He knows the Indian subcontinent and Southeast Asia as well as his pants pocket and holster.

As for Egypt, the crocodiles already whistle his name in front of the pyramids.

Australia? Australia gets on his nerves.

New Zealand, Guyana, Jamaica, Ceylon, the Fiji Islands, Hong Kong, and Malta: ditto.

Fun, thy name is colonies.

Turbulent days followed in Marlborough House, until it occurred to the prince: Canada wouldn't be half bad.

Canada!

An icy gust blows in from the Rocky Mountains, and mustangs and buffalo graze on the prairies. And there are farms everywhere, trappers ahoy.

An order was placed by telegraph for the Prince of Wales: a ranch, a real Canadian ranch, the kind the wild guys over there live in, pieced together out of gnarled wooden tree trunks, rough and weatherproof, thousands of miles from Quebec and Montreal, in the midst of immense forests and endless prairies. A simple ranch with six bathrooms, two billiards rooms, a bridge room, a dance hall, three bars, and so on.

Everything according to the prince's own wish list. A steamship full of suitcases departed from England, and there was a big flurry of activity to put together the ranch.

Good summer retreat for a prince.

Daily schedule:

Get up at five-thirty. A little ride on an empty stomach and in a red tailcoat can't hurt.

Seven to eleven: first round of breakfast, English-style. Clothing: pajamas or a green silk bathrobe.

Eleven to two: conversation with the courier. ("Where's my pay?" Forty thousand pounds salary and sixty thousand pounds from the Duchy of Cornwall's income.)

Two to four: light meal outdoors, then press reception. Clothing: cowboy pants, purple shirt, purple tie, purple handkerchief, purple hatband. The prince is clad in purple.

Four to six: reception with the public. Clothing: two-piece outfit, striped trousers, black sports jacket.

Six to eight: *Souper dansant.** For this purpose, two locals wind up the gramophone. The prince gives Black Bottom lessons. A game of billiards. Clothing: tuxedo.

---

* Dinner dance.

Eight to twelve: game of bridge. In nice weather at the foot of the Rocky Mountains. Clothing: tailcoat.

Then dancing.

Newspaper clippings from British newspapers: "Our prince is living among the farmers in Canada."

"Our prince shoots seven buffaloes."

"Our prince wins at breaking in wild horses."

"Our prince gets lost in the mountains."

"Our prince learns how to throw a lasso."

—Recently they woke up the prince, at about three in the morning, to find out whether he might enjoy taking part in a hunt. What kind of question is that? He rode off in his night-shirt. Yes, indeed!

Hello, prince, you are a funny boy.

Now, more than ever, as a genuine trapper.

Berliner Börsen Courier, August 31, 1927

Chaplin II and the Others at the Scala

An excellent program! Colorful, sparkling, and what is more: it's new!

Clowns: there's Will *Cummin*, a magnificent young fellow, who uses an umbrella as a lighter and takes his hat for a stroll balanced on a cigar; who amazes a juggler by working with twelve top hats and thus parodying Rastelli; who pours hundreds of gallons of water out of a paltry little vase, all the while making the sweetest of all silly faces.—And then there is the *Andren* family, musical geniuses, vaudeville virtuosos of the first order. With a little boy whose eyes flicker unending melancholy and fiddles "Träumerei" while slinking along on tiptoe.

Three bears and Okito: One gray bear enters on roller skates to start things off, then a second one tap-dances, and the third (Fräulein Ottilie from Schöneberg, as Joseph *Breker*, the trainer, calls this one) rides a bike. With the grace and ease of young girls. Yes, it is only when the band jazzes things up with a wild Charleston that the three forget their outstanding training. Like lunatics they pull at their chains, to the beat and with syncopation, of course, but in such a spirited manner that they tear Mr. Breker's sidekick's pants to pieces. And *Okito*: an illusionist without a moderator, which is quite an advantage. At the same time, this "Asian" man is a great artist; how does he do the thing with the gold ball and the thing with the geese? The full dozen wonderful kimonos that Okito presents with the refinement of Paris models is already enough to give you your money's worth.

Dance attractions: To be honest, these are a bit weak. We've seen much better modern dance than what Laczi and Änni do.

Chaplin II: Two acrobats, pretty fellows, and Charlie Rivel; that is the troupe. This Rivel is quite consciously doing a copy. But it comes from within, and it's so strong that it's justified. (Justified from a legal standpoint, at any rate, for the very reason that Chaplin, the great one, is no more an original than he is; people say it's Billy Hurrydale, a second-rate British dope.) Rivel is a brilliant observer, he knows genius like the pocket of his threadbare trousers. In his discreet way, he manages to transport Chaplin into the three-dimensional sphere—and pulls it off surprisingly well. It goes without saying that his partners, who perform countless flips, deserve ample praise.

Incredible feats: Someone who calculates the square root of 33,000,262,176! This phenomenon is Emanuel *Steiner*, who plays around effortlessly with twenty-digit numbers; as he says himself, the only person in the world who isn't thrown even by numbers in the billions. He also has an unnerving knowledge of all possible and impossible dates in history; he knows that Archimedes was born on a Thursday; and the result of 766 to the fourth power divided by 77. (A rosy-cheeked skeptic next to me keeps grunting: tour de force; I ought to have him work out my liabilities!)

Someone with gasometer lungs! *Omikron* is a slender blond man in a violet outfit, looking like an ad for a vacuum cleaner. He gulps in enough gas to send off a couple of people into the hereafter with some to spare. He uses this gas to light lamps, heat an iron, cook a fried egg. You wind up with a bitter taste in your mouth, but you're amazed by this fellow, and how!

And someone who goes through the eye of a needle! Martin *Sczeny*, Mexican, with a slight Hungarian intonation; he's barrel chested, and brawny from head to toe. An escape artist, a matador of breaking free. Twenty people from the audience put a straitjacket over his head, then swaddle him like a child in diapers. In one minute he is free. Lifts himself up onto the palms of his hands and does somersaults that make his joints crack with a spine-chilling snap. At the end he crawls through a steel ring no bigger than a soup plate. Gets off to a running start again and again, the ladies storm up from their front-row seats, then: yank, his spinal column bends, again and again, done! Lots of effort, lots of sweat. Bravo!

Berliner Börsen Courier, May 10, 1927

The Lookalike Man

TALE OF A CHAMELEON NAMED ERWIN

The dictionary may define individuals as unique and inimitable, but that doesn't do Erwin one bit of good. The world around him doesn't think in those terms. In flagrant disregard of the scientific definition, it confers on him the dubious ability to multiply. As lazily as the bureau that attaches descriptions to passport applicants, it denies the existence of any "distinguishing marks" he might have, ignores all the specific features of his appearance, and reduces him to a template. Because he is of medium height and has black hair—like Herr Klappke—it takes him for Herr Klappke. Because he wears dark horn-rimmed glasses and has brown eyes—like Herr Rednitz—it takes him for Herr Rednitz. Erwin cannot be Erwin. Fate has destined him to be the victim of the undeveloped physiognomic memory of his fellow men.

Over the years, Erwin has had to play every imaginable role. The roles forced on him range from a grocer's apprentice to a film comedian, from a troubled youth to a cousin gone missing in Australia. At first he vehemently opposed any false identification. He refused to be the one who was supposedly "recognized," and tried to clear up the confusion with denials and a stamped personal identification card. He had yet to learn how obstinately people insist on defending their mistakes. He had yet to foresee the mistrust his protests would sow. No one believed his avowals that he was not the one he had been taken for. If they believed him at all, it was the part that he didn't *want* to be that person, that he had some painful reason to dispute his identity. Soon Erwin's peaceful nature grew tired of the constant squabbling. He acquiesced, and sought to bear his destiny of "looking similar" with dignity. He good-naturedly turned into an unwilling swindler. He let mistakes take their course and strove to conform reasonably well to the roles demanded of him. If threatened with exposure, he would leave on the spot.

Two weeks ago everything was going along smoothly, but then, in a dance hall, a bony monster tried to reclaim Erwin as her bridegroom, who had deserted her before the year was out. Erwin put his foot down. He had been hoping for a pleasant mix-up, and did not have the slightest desire to spend the evening at the side of this skeleton draped in black. He understood at first glance why the groom had fled. So he resorted to denials and displaying his stamped ID card, the way he used to do. A terrible scene ensued right there. The bony bride shouted to everyone that he had already tried this fake papers maneuver once before, though back then his name was *Egon*. If he didn't pony up his alimony back payments right away, she would hand him over to the police. She lunged at him threateningly, and the other guests took her side. Slaps in the face and worse followed.

When Erwin got home in a fit of desperation, his first thought was to grab a razor and slit his wrists. He later realized how little this sort of behavior suited his style. He moaned and groaned all the way till morning, having had quite enough of bearing the burdens of others on top of the heap of misfortune already allotted to himself. Then he came to a decision. No matter what, *he had to* have his own "distinguishing mark." Although he could not revise history, he did have the power to accentuate his individuality, and that is what he would do. He renounced any trace of human vanity.

Now Erwin sports muttonchops and a shaved head. A metal-rimmed pince-nez bobs up and down on his nose. His stand-up collar reaches up to his chin. He wears brown top boots, and a faded Tyrolean hat adorns his head. When he trudges across the street, people nudge one another with a laugh. "Quite an inventive disguise," they say, and muse about who might be trying to hide behind that mask—Herr Klappke or Herr Rednitz?

Berliner Börsen Courier, June 14, 1927

A Minister on Foot

No doubt about it: that's him. That bull neck, the sharp horizontal line of those square shoulders, those determinedly casual steps are unmistakable. Theo has often studied the silhouette of the minister's back in the caricatured exaggerations of the satirical magazines. Even so, he hesitates to vouch for this encounter. A minister on foot, in a business suit? Such an ordinary, inconspicuous part of the procession of afternoon strollers? Full of disdain for all party politics, Theo still has too much respect for high-ranking government officials to picture them without a formal police presence. A newspaper headline he catches sight of in passing dispels his doubts. Oh, I get it, parliamentary session. The minister has given his big speech. Understandably, he is looking for a break in the fresh air after the contentious debates. Five steps behind him, Theo glides through the summer evening in the ministerial wake.

No one pays much attention to the rarely seen flâneur and his daydreaming appendage. If this event were announced officially, the gawking crowd would soon be pushing and shoving en masse. But today, as he is not expected, let alone in such an unaccustomed procession, not one of the thousands recognizes the statesman. "Our surest form of incognito," Theo notes down for his little book of aphorisms, "is the undeveloped physiognomic memory of our fellow men." On a refreshing break from his usual dignified stance, he could relax and tuck his left hand playfully into the back tab of his overcoat while his right arm swings back and forth happily. The embodiment of the foreign office is strolling right in front of Theo's probing gaze. A pleasant young man at the official's side eagerly chats away to score points with him while leaning in a bit too confidentially, and wearing clothing too exaggeratedly elegant for Theo to regard him as an undersecretary; this is probably his personal secretary.—What might the two of them be so absorbed in discussing? Tidbits from a cabinet session? The plan for a new political initiative? An overpowering desire to find out makes Theo forget to keep his distance. Inadvertently, his pace quickens, and his arm almost brushes against the man in front of him. His ears lie in wait for state secrets. "Yes, my dear," he hears the minister say, "in the end, this will be a real summer." Nothing else, a long pause.

Disappointed, Theo pulls back to his earlier position. Frankly, he expected more. He had no need to eavesdrop on a minister's conversation for the sake of such banal truth. At every moment, with every word, a politician of this stature ought to be aware of his obligation to focus on significant matters. Still, he takes solace in the knowledge that it could have been worse. After all, at least it was a full sentence. A statement, even. "Real summer." Up to this point, that had been by no means certain. Now it has become a fact. He had it from the best source. Officially, you might say. Feeling better about the whole thing, Theo decides to hang on. After all, he has nothing to lose by investing a few more minutes. His thoughts revolve around the experience, and he starts to process the scene. *Dress rehearsal for the report in the café. Those envious glances . . . The minister recognized me right away, requested that I accompany him. Ostensibly only the conventional chitchat about the weather. But with a hidden agenda. Meteorology and politics. It'll get dry and warm, so the British-Russian conflict will have to . . .* A sudden downpour jolts Theo out of his fantasies. He rushes for cover in a hallway to keep his flimsy outfit dry, while the minister, discounted so precipitously, dodges any complications by fleeing the scene.

Berliner Börsen Courier, July 7, 1927

Interview with a Witch

WOMEN'S NEWEST PROFESSION

The card lying before me, with its delicate copperplate engraving and refined type, struck me as nearly incomprehensible: *Magda C. offers her services in performing metaphysical missions.* Metaphysical missions? What are those? Was this about communicating with the dead, mediumistic matters? Was Magda C. a medium using the path of spiritualist science? What did she do? Who was she and what did she look like? Whatever the case, this could open a little hidden door into the realm of marvels, coolly and unemotionally. On the face of it, Magda C. was not a pallid theosophist on the brink of cringeworthy raptures. The trendy design of the business card made that quite evident. Clear objectivity shone through, training in the methods of meeting modern demands. I called her up and invited her over for a visit.

A young, well-attired lady, looking quite distinguished, showed up, sat down in an armchair, and began: "I am Magda C.; my last name doesn't matter. It is totally clear to me, of course, that you're unable to picture anything specific in regard to metaphysical missions. My field—or, if I may put it this way, my profession—requires a brief explanation. You undoubtedly know that we are living in a metaphysically minded age, in spite of all the talk about crass materialism and so forth . . ."

"Certainly! But won't you tell me right from the start, without any special introduction, what your metaphysical missions consist of? What do you actually do?"

"I wish," she stated simply. "Nothing more than that. I accept commissions from the well-to-do to make wishes.—Wishes, intensely cultivated, intervene in the course of events. Wishes have power. But most people are powerless, or too lethargic, to wish for themselves. I make myself available to people like that for a moderate fee with my tried-and-true wishing power. I integrate their wishes into my schedule and wish for them, intensely and confidently. They are unburdened, depression drains away from their souls, they can go to the theater, to a concert, to balls, with the reassuring feeling that their issues, their wishes, are in the care of an experienced professional . . ."

"So what do you wish for, Madam? Perhaps some examples."

"Mostly death and destruction," she said, with a friendly smile. "Loss of assets, loss of face, and a bit of damage. For one person I wish for someone to defraud a business, for another I wish for a minor but annoying skin disease. The wishes, especially those of my female clients, get quite elaborate. Loss of a piece of jewelry, hair loss, rapid weight gain—think of that as my bread-and-butter work. There are people who have read older books of magic, have trained with Eliphas Lévi or Papus and consequently cling to a strict ceremonial. I don't think much of that, but I let them have their fun. They hand over photographs of their enemies, instruct me to pierce them with a gold needle or to put a hex on little wax figures that symbolically represent their adversaries. The main point remains concentration, focusing the will squarely on the goal."

"And are you successful? I mean: are your wishes fulfilled, or rather, those of your clients? Can you earn a living from your odd profession?"

She made an elegant sweeping motion with her hand. "Take a look around you! Don't you see people everywhere on the street talking loudly to themselves, gesticulating with their hands? What are these people doing? They're wishing. Fervently! Ardently! Wishing for death and destruction, misery and meltdown. They believe in the destructive power of their wishes, take comfort in it, and gain the courage to face life. Don't you think that's a vital need just crying out for gratification? Which can be the focus of an adequate business? How about the women who tell fortunes using a deck of cards? That's surely no different. In earlier times, people were content just to put a curse on the milk of a cow or to cast a spell on the fields. Life has become more multifaceted; the opportunities have expanded. You've got trade, industry, a monetized economy. But the human soul has essentially remained the same. You can call me a modern witch if you like . . ."

She took out her compact and a mirror and applied some rouge to her cheeks.

"You won't believe me on all this," she continued, "but what I am telling you is absolutely true. I have put the so-called chasms of the soul to good use. The first time it was a joke, a whim. At a gathering I offered my services in jest, wishing, on behalf of a busy business tycoon, for his enemy to have a car accident. Two days later, it came true. Word got around. People I didn't know came to my apartment in secret, and carefully felt their way into conversations about the accident. They told me I had been recommended to them, they would like to . . . one could . . . occult influences . . . metaphysical missions. I knew enough. Today I make a living from this."

"And your conscience?"

"Criminal charges would never stick. Witchcraft no longer counts as a crime in our oddly enlightened age, even though I think that over time a provision on this issue will need to be reinstated in the penal code. And theoretically, the effect is truly the same whether I'm the one doing the wishing or my clients are. Basically the whole thing comes down to what you believe . . ."

"Can you show me a list of your clients?"

"No, discretion obviously prevents me from doing that. But you'd be amazed at what sorts of people seek me out. People who occupy prominent positions in public life. People in banking who call on me to use my power for complex and difficult transactions. Big businessmen who want to have me wish for the success of their new product. Every Monday I'm invited to visit the general manager of a major industrial group, who swears by my supernatural powers and makes use of them for all his businesses. You're skeptical, amazed, taken aback. But in two, three weeks, I'm certain I'll be counting you among my clients, too. Don't resist! There's no point. You'll come around. I know it. It makes too much sense nowadays, meshes too well with people's current psychological conditions, with the situation as a whole. The modern witch is a necessary sign of the times . . ."

This young, good-looking, elegant, highly sophisticated lady actually exists. I really and truly did talk with her, she sat in my apartment, chatting away as though it was the most natural thing in the world. And I think it's worth noting, for cultural and historical reasons, that a witch was able to establish herself in 1927 and do well enough in her profession to live more than comfortably. Her clothing was definitely from a top-notch boutique.

Berliner Börsen Courier, October 23, 1927

Grock, the Man Who Makes the World Laugh

A melancholy man goes to a famous doctor and tells his tales of woe. The doctor gives him this advice: "Go see Debureau the clown—if he can't get you to laugh, you're a lost cause." The man shakes his head. "I can't go see Debureau; I *am* Debureau!"

His gray-checked trousers are so baggy that they're swimming on him like a loose scarf, he is sweating so much that his makeup is dripping from his temples and nose, his ridiculously hulking shoes seem as heavy as lead balls, his back is crooked. This is how Grock comes into the dressing room—a sad old man.

Outside, a thousand hands are clapping, the sound of laughter can be heard all the way over here, Grock had twelve curtain calls, and flowers, so many flowers.

Grock, the man, plops down on the chair in the corner and breathes heavily. They wipe the sweat off his face. He can no longer keep his eyes open; that's how much the footlights have blinded him. The photographer who has been waiting for an hour asks him to pose. Grock pulls his lips, which are painted black, into such a wide grimace that they almost touch his earlobes, and he grins into the lens. I think he dozes off during the photo sessions. But he doesn't have the guts to say: Do it fast, that's enough laughing, I have to get to bed!

Grock, the clown who has to make the world laugh, wants to get to bed, he doesn't want to keep posing, he doesn't want to smile, he wants to sleep!

Bienne is a small German city in Switzerland. Clock factories, clockmakers, clockface designers, clock hands manufacturers. And a café, *Zum Paradies*, owned by Herr Wettach, son, and daughter. Business at the café is as bad as bad can be, the people in Bienne are so hardworking. So what does Karl, the ten-year-old son, do about it? He performs in Papa's café, juggles with cheesecake and beer bottles, plays the harmonica, tells the joke about the hippo and the sewing machine. The café is now full, every single evening, because his sister has also become an amateur performer, dancing on the rope stretched between the buffet and the cloakroom. Wettach has talented kids.

But the two develop an appetite for the circus ring, run away, find a spot for themselves with the circus, travel the world. Still, Karl Wettach is far from being Grock. First he lifts hefty weights, then he plays the clarinet, then he drops this career path and becomes a language teacher. Goes back to the circus. Successes, always successes. And the next thing you know, he is Grock, the clown dictator, the man who is booked solid for three years—his pay is guaranteed.

Eighteen years ago Grock was in Berlin. Came from Zirkus Schumann, went to the Wintergarten. Partner: Antonet. So what happened? Antonet and Grock bombed, because there is an enormous difference between the stage and the circus ring.— Antonet and Grock reworked the act, and one week later they—along with Reutter—were one of the two top attractions in Berlin.

His name is Grock, and here's why: Brick, a very popular music clown, lost his partner, Brock, when Brock died. Then he looked for a new partner. Found Karl Wettach. They made a contract. But Brick and Brock had such a good name that Brick asked Wettach to call himself Brock. Wettach didn't want to, since he never adorns himself with borrowed plumes. He called himself Grock. The name has stuck to this day.

What props does Grock work with?

He plays the piano, saxophone, miniature violin, and accordion.

He can dance a little, he can juggle a little, he can do a little gymnastics.

That is all.

There are performers who can present all these little odds and ends with so much humanity. There are no performers who do comedy as profoundly as Grock. He is a *clown of the soul*, a metaphysical clown, as it were.

There is no performer who can replicate that, there is none.

Except one: Chaplin.

Chaplin and Grock are two brilliant brothers. Somewhere, deep down within them, their individualities connect.

It is said of Mark Twain that while concocting his droll stories in bed, he always wept, and that Saphir thought of his best punch lines during his strolls at a cemetery in Vienna. Chaplin read Greek philosophy.

And Grock, the clown, has gray hair and *suuuch* a sad face.

The only one who could entertain Grock is Grock. Grock would laugh until he cried about Grock.

Berliner Börsen Courier, November 2, 1927

Ten Minutes with Chaliapin

Such a commotion.

A hundred bellboys. Elevator up, elevator down. All the top management. Everyone in the film industry. Fountain pens scratching away. Cameras eating up plate after plate. A camera takes aim, menacing as a cannon. The heavy hand of a portly cartoonist is trembling. Everyone is sweating.

My God, my God.

Just a bunch of people: a manager who looks like Feodor Chaliapin, and a Chaliapin who appears to be a heavyweight wrestler.

Only his head. A fine, good, noble head. Unmoving. Like the Volga (a short, wizened-looking lady, in spite of her youth, said as much in the hallway, while lovingly clutching a volume of Turgenev to her Persian fur and somehow treating her words as a pitch for the first topic).

But Feodor: a warm little wool jacket over the world's most expensive bass voice; green tie, the red cockade of the Legion of Honor on his lapel; drinks sherry and speaks the broad French of someone who never makes it past the novice level; his hair is fair as flax; the cigar he is smoking seems to be the very best import, Chaliapin's broad chest inhales its smoke deeply, too deeply; the singer's fans are starting to stare.

From the crossfire that keeps coming at him, and which he withstands patiently, like a pro, we learn:

That Feodor Chaliapin was born in Kazan, in Tatarstan;

That his parents, simple peasants that they were, worked the land and had a warm pechka, a warm stove at which the young Feodor dreamed of Nevsky Prospect and the Iberian mother of God;

That Chaliapin joined a boys' choir through divine providence, and in this post he got nothing less than one ruble per month;

That Feodor, who was smitten by the world of the stage at the tender age of twelve, traveled throughout the hinterlands of Russia at seventeen as a funny old man in a ludicrous operetta;

That in Tiflis, in the Caucasus, Chaliapin finally devoted himself wholeheartedly to his voice training, while his teacher, Usatov, spared neither effort nor cost to rein him in;

Then just like that, Feodor was hired to perform in Petersburg and Moscow at the Imperial Opera, and the rest was smooth sailing.

"*C'est ma vie*," Chaliapin stated, and toasted every second year of his development, which he recounted bit by bit, with a sip of sherry; today he is up to fifty-two.

Never have I known that there could be so many questions. What would Chaliapin's aunt have named her son if it had been up to him? And what about the everlasting nature of art? Isn't it really about time for them to straighten out the Leaning Tower of Pisa? The pay, how much? And so forth.

He raved about Toscanini and Rachmaninoff and others. But Wagner, on the other hand, was not for him, you know—

The conversation turned to Soviet Russia. Chaliapin hadn't been there for five years. Those on the right wanted firm proof that he was against his homeland. Those on the left latched onto everything positive Chaliapin had to say about Moscow.

It seemed to me that Feodor was celebrating his brothers fervently, though at a distance. But I didn't speak my mind.

Ate only caviar, genuine Astrachan caviar. Went down the stairs and whistled softly—out of reverence, I suppose—the burlaks' song, "*Ej Uchnem*" [i.e., from *Song of the Volga Boatmen*]. *Da svidania, gospodin* Feodor!

Berliner Börsen Courier, November 12, 1927

Claude Anet in Berlin

Yesterday I met Monsieur Claude Anet on the Esplanade, and I have to say that I don't know what you want from him; I find him very serious. When I happened to bring up the subject of Anita Loos, her *Gentlemen Prefer Blondes*, I thought I saw a furrow forming on Claude Anet's pleasant forehead; he resented my mentioning him in the same breath as Dekobra and other popular writers. He's right, of course, because he is in the business of literature and takes it quite seriously.

We should not, of course, misconstrue that. Anet is not the man of letters we take him to be. One topic we spoke about was the German novel, but alas, Anet had only this to say, in an extraordinarily charming manner—naturally—that apart from Goethe he knows only one single German: Dr. Peltzer, whom he saw running at the Stade de Colombes, and that it was simply *formidable* how the German outran Séra Martin.

Anet's enthusiasm for the sport is quite touching. After all, he himself was a French tennis champion for years! And he put

Suzanne Lenglen, the queen of tennis, on a pedestal. Sports and women are two topics that appeal to him in equal measure.

Anet, French and of noble descent, born at Lake Geneva, studied at the Sorbonne in Paris and earned his teaching certificate, yet he never practiced the profession. He wrote. When a Frenchman writes, he writes about love, in a hundred out of a hundred cases. He spent some time in Russia as a correspondent for the *Petit Parisien*, and even though there was a revolution in progress, he found enough time to fall head over heels in love with the Russian women. It was here that he wrote *Ariane*, which brought Anet fame. He continues to write about love and women; heaven knows he never runs out of material. But the women requite his love; his *Notes sur Amour* are on the night tables of the madams, in London and in Prague, in Paris and in Berlin.

I will leave the closing words to Claude Anet himself:

"The lady-killer disappears after his victory. Then the women curse the hour he was born, yet they regret not that he came, but that he went."

Berliner Börsen Courier, November 25, 1927

At the Home of the Oldest Woman in Berlin

Frau Auguste Richter, Berlin-Moabit, Birckenstr. 30, is celebrating her one-hundredth birthday today. The Berlin magistrate, Zörgiebel, the police chief of Berlin, and many other officials showed up in their capacity as well-wishers.

The birthday girl who is the object of the excitement in Moabit today, with all conversations revolving around her and flowers and little heartfelt gifts delivered here, is lying in a snow-white bed, her toothless mouth in a smile, training her beady eyes, red-rimmed but alert, on each intruder as if to say, I'm happy you're happy that today's my one-hundredth birthday.

They've put a hundred things in Frau Richter's room: porcelain cups, real pure coffee, lace hankies, chocolates, candies, prayer books with ivory covers, and a silk scarf. The door to Frau Helene Wendlers, the daughter of the woman who's turned a hundred, doesn't stop opening, and everyone is there to see the marvel: the oldest woman in Berlin.

Frau Auguste Richter is actually an exception in her family. Her father "only" made it to age sixty-five, her mother "only" to age eighty-four. She has spent her entire life in Moabit, where she was also born. She still has a sister in Berlin, who is all of eighty-eight and may be well on her way to beating Auguste's record.

Grandchildren play ring-around-the-rosy around their hundred-year-old grandmother's bed, she always laughs, pulls her hands out from under the blanket—slender, wax-colored hands full of wrinkles, but still strong—and claps out the beat. And downstairs in the courtyard, someone plays on the guitar:

We'll never meet again while we're so young
It'll never be so wonderful again . . .

Berliner Börsen Courier, December 9, 1927

Felix Holländer

ON HIS SIXTIETH BIRTHDAY

The latest to turn sixty years old is Felix Holländer, who will join these ranks tomorrow, in a series of milestones among the generation once called "naturalist," which started with Gerhart

Hauptmann, Max Halbe, and Otto Erich Hartleben. Holländer was one of the first in line. He launched his career in the newspaper business, dealing with the restlessness of the day in a way that requires the sharpest vigilance. Like Hauptmann, he is Silesian. In one of his best novels, he portrayed the middle-class patriarchal sphere of his childhood home, and in *Dream and Day* he depicted nature and the villages of the Riesengebirge.

In the early 1890s he became a novelist in Berlin. A collapse of a bank, Unter den Linden, was the subject of his *Tempest in the West*, a portrait of society framed with a keen eye for current events, which was one of the first to capture the abrupt shifts that occurred during this transitional period, its crises, and its sensations. Then Holländer wrote *Jesus and Judas*, a novel of the socialist movement. And at the end of the decade his major novel of personal development, *The Path of Thomas Truck*, recapitulated everything that was being debated among intellectuals.

Thomas Truck, who yearns to take the cares of the world upon himself and whose idealism is seduced and duped by the sensuality of a millionaire's wife from the Tiergarten neighborhood, meets a working-class girl at a Salvation Army gathering. The suicide of this poor soul, who has sunk so low, inspires him to regain his freedom. In the bohemian group that gathers at the "Nachtlicht," he is drawn to all kinds of revolutionary inclinations and finds the balance he is seeking in a Tolstoyan Christ. This novel has secured its place even today in the history of novels that depict the era between 1900 and the present.

From then on Felix Holländer remained one of the most widely read storytellers, often astounding his readers with the sure touch he gave his characters, and always with the nervous art of tension, as in *The Oath of Stefan Huller*, set in the milieu of acrobats in a variety show, and in *The Dancer*, the fantastically crafted novel of a con man.

His foray into playwriting resulted in a single stage drama, *Ackermann*, which he co-scripted with Lothar Schmidt and which enjoyed success onstage with Emanuel Reicher in the lead role. But he always had a secret love for the theater itself. He pursued this love when Max Reinhardt was working in Berlin, approaching him as a dramaturge and director, and for many years was the energy behind the operation, with tremendous vitality and stamina that only increased as time went on. When Reinhardt left the Deutsches Theater, Holländer took over the directorship and stayed in this post throughout the chaos of the postwar years until the worst was over and he could once again place it in Reinhardt's hands. Now he's back in the theater critic's orchestra seat. In addition, he did sparkling work as a stage producer.

Perhaps he has thought of writing a memoir by this point. He was invariably in the thick of every moment of turmoil. It would surely be very interesting if he were to portray a portion of his journey, because he would be speaking not only of personal matters but of a turbulent era in the history of Berlin.

B. Z. am Mittag, October 31, 1927

The Elder Statesman of Berlin Theater Critics

ON THE DEATH OF ALFRED KLAAR

Alfred Klaar, the elder statesman of Berlin theater critics, who has now died two days before completing his seventy-ninth year of life, began his life on Prague soil, just like Fritz Mauthner. He taught at the Deutsche Technik academy, where he acquired the title of professor. He served as theater critic for the *Bohemia*. He was a focal point in the intellectual life of the city, in which he gave the final outdoor speech in German at a Schiller commemoration. To this day there is a picture of Klaar hanging in the rooms of the Concordia, the Prague writers' association, for which he organized the talks. He looks like a mild-mannered, dark-bearded, pensive individual.

As a critic, Klaar embraced the aesthetics of idealism. For him, the German classical drama was the eternal high point; he wrote extended essays on *Maria Stuart* and reviews in serial form. But because he was at home in the Austrian cultural sphere, he enjoyed early exposure to the world of Ludwig Anzengruber, and with every generation he progressed into the next one.

The best thing about him was the forbearance with which he adapted to trends that had to have been unfamiliar to him. The criticism he penned at an advanced age was gentle and well intentioned. In the decades of his professional life he had seen a great deal, starting in Prague, at Angelo Neumann's German Theater, where the luminaries of the north German and Austrian theater gathered as guests and for many a future giant of the theater was the springboard to success. He had a comprehensive overview of talents and trends, and in addition to his ability to recognize individual strengths, he was well versed in his capacity as a patriarch.

When he moved to the capital of the German Empire with Paula Eberty, a Berlin actress who worked with Else Lehmann, he wrote for the *Berliner Neueste Nachrichten*, then for the *Vossische Zeitung*, Theodor Fontane's and Paul Schlenther's newspaper. He kept on working tirelessly right into his days of infirmity, and he attended every premiere, in a misbuttoned black tailcoat, a friendly old man with bright, serious eyes. The Association of Berlin Theater Critics just recently named him honorary president.

Of all of Alfred Klaar's books, one stands out as the full expression of his personality. Its title is *We and Humanity*. This literary historian, who also wrote an account of Spinoza's philosophy, was a humane individual to the depths of his soul. One of his last publications was a study of Heinrich von Kleist's *Marquise of O.* He was a highly enthusiastic orator and had an astonishing memory. Anyone who has heard him talk about someone like Uriel Acosta for more than an hour without any notes knows his integrity and his ethical stance, and his exacting mastery of the word will ensure people's reverential love for him well into the future.

B. Z. am Mittag, November 5, 1927

The *B. Z.* Lady and the German Crown Prince

At two on the dot, Schappel goes into Taubenschlag Restaurant on Behrenstrasse, sets up shop in the corner, spreads out at the round table in the back, and adjusts her cap, making the yellow knitted Latin letters *B* and *Z*, the newspaper's famous acronym, run diagonally across her forehead, and as Frau Schappel pulls a good deal of change out of her coat pocket with her right hand, she presses her broad left thumb against her left nostril, which has a whole network of fine red veins running across it, like rivers on a map, while blowing a lungful of air through the other nostril. This is Frau Schappel's way of regulating her breathing rhythms—then she lifts her head slightly and calls over to the bar: "Erna, a cuppa coffee!"

It's been that way for twenty-five years. Erna serves Frau Luise Schappel four cups of coffee a day, which add up to four times twenty-five, that is, 100 times 365, 36,500 coffees all told, and then the leap years need to be added on, and Sundays and holidays subtracted. On those days Frau Schappel doesn't sell the

B. Z.; she lies in bed on Brunnenstrasse until three o'clock, ventilating her vocal cords, and only here and there do words burst forth, when Frau Schappel argues with her husband about who holds the record in selling the magazine. "He hawks 'em now, too. He needed a do-over, seeing as he was once a radical comedian, yes indeed. He has the same name as Stresemann."

Gustav?

"Nah, Gus. But he's still a beginner. I've been at it for twenty-five years, starting in 1904. Until 1904 I sold flowers, on Unter den Linden. Who still buys flowers, I ask you? Do you know the local barber Gilbert's shop at the corner of Exerzierstrasse and Kanonierstrasse, I've been there the whole time. You know, neither storms nor rain nor heat nor frost. What's it down to today. Forty-five. That's nothin'. In 1917 it was up to seventy, but your hanky still froze to your face, in 1910 I almost lost my mind and passed out, and in the fall we can never dry off. We deal with so much crap just to keep you in the know."

Once again Frau Schappel presses her thumb against her left nostril, emitting a strangely booming sound, the kind a broken saxophone might make. After a big gulp of coffee, she begins to sort through the pile of money with the tip of her index finger peeking out of her torn black glove; her finger and the glove are the exact same color: the half-groschens with the half-groschens, the groschens with the groschens, and the marks with the marks. Whenever she comes across a three-mark coin, she shakes her weighty head and says, "Back then I got a taler!"—and everyone at the Taubenschlag instantly knows what's coming.

Here is the story of the crown prince and the taler:

It was 1914, in April or May, not a hint of war as yet, when he came riding along in his coach, from the general staff's offices on Leipziger Strasse, down Behrenstrasse, to the castle. Sitting next to him was his adjutant, Mühlenberg, Mühlenreich,

Mühlendorf, or something of that sort. Frau Schappel saw the coach coming, recognized the crown prince, and began to wave newspapers around, the way Robinson had with his nightshirt when he saw the first ship sail past his island.

Then it got even better: the crown prince stopped—on my honor—right in front of Frau Luise Schappel, the adjutant handed the crown prince a taler, and the crown prince handed it on to Frau Schappel, Frau Schappel handed him a B. Z., as she stood there trembling with fear and feeling ill, and stammered out, "Thank you very much, His Highness, Crown Prince!" The crown prince gave her quite a nice wave, and the coach disappeared. This pattern repeated every day.

Frau Schappel had been instructed by the adjutant, who went to Gilbert's to get shaved, not to address the crown prince as "His Highness, Crown Prince," but rather simply as "Imperial Majesty," and she needed to "step lively." Alas, our Lieschen really wanted to step lively, but when he showed up, Frau Schappel grew red as a beet and kept on saying, "His Highness, Crown Prince."

Yes, those were nice times for Frau Schappel, she knew that he bought the newspaper "just for fun," because "he never ever reads," surely he made his daily trips along Behrenstrasse for her sake, Frau Schappel was less interested in the taler. But she soon figured out for herself that, no, he didn't come just on account of Frau Schappel: over at no. 58, the address of the Friedrich Wilhelm Life Insurance office, the telephone receptionists lined up at the window, day after day, all dolled up, waiting for him excitedly.

Frau Schappel had an idea why he bought the newspaper from her every day: her newspaper stand was straight across from the windows where fifty girls with bright-red little faces hung there like ripe grapes, and Frau Schappel was already forty years old. She was overcome with jealousy.

Well, and then the war came, and that was that.

Frau Schappel drinks her third coffee today, remarks that the papers from Bolivia and Paraguay are now selling well, she talks about her best days, about the sinking of the *Titanic*, about the first weeks of the war, about Fritz Haarmann and Charles Lindbergh and Krantz and the Zeppelin blimp. Meanwhile, one drop after another splashes out of Frau Schappel's nose right between the half-groschens and groschens sorted neatly on the tabletop.

Der Querschnitt, issue 2, February 1929

Stroheim, the Man We Love to Hate

His name is "Von," pure and simple, and nowadays every child in Hollywood knows who "Von" is. Erich von Stroheim, that was too cumbersome. They pulled the "Von" out of his name and are inordinately fond of calling him that exclusively, as though wishing to flaunt the three noble letters on this playground for parvenus, and they pronounce this "Von" like "one." And if a Hollywood greenhorn should ask, "Why do you call Stroheim 'one'?"—the answer is: because every company can shoot only one film with him, then it goes broke.

That's the great thing about Stroheim: for fifteen years he bankrupts the studio; for fifteen years they throw millions at him, again and again; saying nothing when he tinkers with a film for years, which he then abruptly drops when he finds it tedious; watching patiently as he spends six weeks working on a single love scene, the length of which, just between us, is twelve yards; paying a ton of money to the stars, extras, and studio workers, everyone runs around for a whole month without doing anything, just because "Von" isn't in the right mood yet.

Even so, they hold onto Stroheim—the way they would hold onto cactuses or decadent wind chimes. Out of respect for his unique skills, people even buy into his moods. They don't let him go. Perhaps they're ashamed of being surrounded by so much levelheadedness. But now we have Chaplin and "Von," two geniuses full of caprices and quirks—marvelous, isn't it? Just like in Europe.

*

Stroheim came to America even before the war. He doesn't say why. He was previously an active-duty Austrian officer. Once he was in New York, he had to adapt somewhat: Stroheim debuted in America as a flypaper salesman in Newark. A few months later he was balancing goulash at the Little Hungarian Restaurant on the infamous Houston Street. Then he laid railroad ties and struggled along as a worker while heading west, where he eventually became a ferryman on Lake Tahoe in northern California. In the south, just a few dozen miles away, so to speak, Hollywood was springing up, and cash was flowing.

His ascent can be summed up in a few words. A film company comes to Lake Tahoe. Stroheim gets involved, earns money in the easiest possible way, the camera thing appeals to him, he joins up with this group and goes to Hollywood. David Wark Griffith is in the middle of shooting a film called *Old Heidelberg*. Stroheim's face is a wonderful fit: he plays an extra as a student in a dueling fraternity. One day, there's an argument in the studio: Griffith is not happy with the medals. Stroheim comes forward, expertly sketches genuine Heidelberg medals, and is promoted on the spot to the position of technical adviser at three times the pay. Then Griffith uses him as an actor in *Hearts of the World*, with Stroheim playing a German officer. For the first time he creates a merciless character, which makes a stronger statement against war and militarism than a thousand words. In America a catchphrase is attached to Stroheim's officer: *the man you love to hate*. In Germany he is branded a turncoat, a traitor, a warmonger.

•

Stroheim is in front of Carl Laemmle, the almighty man at Universal: *Let me make a movie, I need five thousand dollars.* An American would have laughed in his face: megalomaniacal extra! Laemmle is a German. Having an Austrian stand before him and come up with plans, brimming with enthusiasm at his own prowess—Laemmle feels sparks fly. He offers the money, the five thousand dollars. And throws in another thirty thousand on top of that. That was the cost of Stroheim's first film, *Blind Husbands.* Stroheim edits the film. Shows it to Laemmle. The editing screen screams out new and original material. All conventions turned upside down. Everything gone about differently. Laemmle shakes his head: *Dear Stroheim, you're five years ahead of us!*

But he gives him money once again. Stroheim makes *The Devil's Pass Key*, then *Foolish Wives.* Script, direction, lead actor: Stroheim. Always as an officer, an Austrian, a Russian. Always *the man you love to hate. Foolish Wives* cost one million dollars. Mangled versions are released in Berlin. Audiences laugh. Stroheim continues to be called a warmonger, and a fool to boot. Stroheim begins work on *Merry-Go-Round* over in the States, reconstructing the whole Prater from Vienna. Longing for his homeland is eating away at him. So as a consolation, he can at least re-create its setting. . . . He doesn't finish shooting the film. Leaves Laemmle for Metro-Goldwyn-Mayer. Makes *Greed.*

Greed runs for exactly one day at the Ufa-Palast am Zoo. Never has there been this kind of film scandal in Berlin. People are aghast that he is five years ahead of us. Independent of the Russians, he uses the Russian style before they do. He foresees something along the lines of visual editing and montage. Shoots in associations. And exposes for the first time: this is how a wedding is in reality, this is a funeral. Sternheim? No, those are

George Grosz characters, their brutal trains of thought written all over their faces. Those fascinate Stroheim!

Stroheim had his first major critical success with *The Merry Widow*. A box office success as well, his only one. His next-to-last film, *The Wedding March*, cost millions. Disaster lies ahead: they get "Von," write up a contract, he swears by all that is holy to spend no more than five hundred thousand dollars and not to shoot any longer than three months. And the moment he has the megaphone back in his hand and sits in the director's chair again, he forgets all that. Can't get past the details. Erich Pommer tells us that he shoots one kiss for six weeks. . . . The lime-tree blossoms that have to fall onto the kissing couple fail to fall just so. The producers grumble but keep coughing up money. Often "Von" pays for the retakes out of his own pocket, like a rich dilettante! Thousands of yards are used up, with whole streets built up, then torn down again. Chaplin—the eternally seeking, experimenting, critical Chaplin—is purposefulness personified in comparison with Stroheim. "Von" turns the studio upside down. Then another director is brought in, who finishes up filming the thing in a mad rush. Just get it done.

Even so, working with him works out. The last film, *Queen Kelly*, with Gloria Swanson, took only ten weeks! They cleverly had the contract read: Stroheim gets one hundred thousand dollars for the manuscript and direction. But the film has to be finished within ten weeks, or else the additional shooting comes at Stroheim's expense. And finished it was, one day before the deadline. Swanson played a madam at a brothel; the film is said to be magnificent. (Incidentally, there *was* a falling-out later on: Stroheim refused to reshoot a sound film insert, because he took a dim view of Movietone. Trial with Swanson. Edmund Goulding, from *Anna Karenina*, makes the sound film scene.)

*

Stroheim is a poor man. DeMille, Griffith, Lubitsch don't know what to do with their money. Murnau bought himself a yacht and wants to spend a year cruising between Japan and California. Stroheim and his family live in a simple little house, and he drives a four-cylinder car. The pure fool of Hollywood.

People who come from Hollywood report that Stroheim wants to go home, but he lacks the courage: how will he be received in Germany?

Der Querschnitt, issue 4, April 1929

A Poker Artist

THE MAGIC OF FRITZ HERRMANN

There ought to be a corporation designed to give this odd man the opportunity to play poker one single time in Palm Beach with Ford, Rockefeller, Vanderbilt: after this evening the corporation would wind up owning the Detroit Automobile Company and the largest fortune in the world. In response to your objection that this corporation would be financing a card shark, I must state that the man—the poker genius—would have no objections to twenty detectives observing the game in slow motion. Nothing would be pinned on him, even if he had four of a kind or flushes each and every time. The eyes of the wary observers would not keep up with the tempo at which he wields his sleight-of-hand techniques. And he is quicker and better at wielding them than anyone in the whole world. Even though at the age of seventy—a milestone he reached back in March—a person's fingers do tremble a bit.

His name is *Fritz Herrmann*, Herrmann with two *r*'s and two *n*'s, and he is the owner of a delicatessen on the north side of Berlin. Skinny children from the Wedding neighborhood press their freckled noses against the display window, where raspberry sweets are lined up, glistening like a mirage, far out of reach. There is also laundry detergent for sale, along with vinegar and gherkins pickled with mustard seeds; in the corner there is a dusty pyramid of bouillon cubes, all neat and tidy. The shop is managed by Frau Herrmann; it doesn't interest him at all. But he is lovingly devoted to the wine cellar under the shop, a superb collection of the rarest labels, which Herrmann, like someone collecting stamps, has acquired using the proceeds from his sorcery. The most esteemed households in Berlin buy their supplies here, Uncle Herrmann carries the fanciest labels, and he is especially proud of the Austrian wines: Vöslauer, Gumpoldskirchner, vintages now available only in bottles.

The Monte Castello isn't bad either, a red "border wine," says Uncle Herrmann, "it doesn't have the dryness of Bordeaux or the sweetness of Spanish wine." We're sitting in a room facing out onto the courtyard, behind the shop, and whenever someone comes into the store and wants to buy something, the bell rings, though it rarely does so. (Any sympathy with the shop owner must be rejected out of hand at this point: Herrmann is a filthy-rich man, who couldn't care less whether he sells any laundry detergent; he keeps the shop for the sake of amusement.) It is eleven o'clock in the morning. We're playing poker. What better thing could one do at this hour? I have picked up a new game and shuffle the cards thoroughly. The room smells a bit musty, but the Monte Castello is extraordinary. I give the shuffled cards to my partner, who holds them between two fingers for half a second, then hands them back to me: "You deal!" I deal, one to him, one to me, each gets five cards. He doesn't even look at his hand, pours himself more red wine, and says in passing, "I lead!" I've placed my cards in a pile and slowly and niftily fan them out, another king, so in any case at least three of a kind, not a bad hand. I keep on spreading out my cards: a fourth king!, and the nine of diamonds. So I have an excellent hand, four kings. The only thing that could beat me would be four aces or a royal flush, that is, five of one suit in sequence. "How many do you want?" I ask Herrmann, who keeps on drinking and hasn't even examined his hand yet. "None!" Heavens, what could he have? Full house? Flush? Straight? That's all too little. Perhaps he has a royal flush? I can't imagine he'd have that much luck. I exchange one card for show, examine it with interest, as though I could still come by a fifth king. I'm actually sorry that we're not playing for money, I would raise him—outbid him—until he folds. But since we're not even playing for peanuts, I reveal my hand with a laugh. As of this moment, he still hasn't seen his hand. He looks at my four kings and calmly announces: "Too little!" Slowly he turns over his cards: four aces. While holding the shuffled cards between his fingers for that half-second, he carried out the crucial sleight of hand. The major poker games in Berlin, the ones whose players have yet to meet Herrmann, ought to be warned about him: you can lose your shirt to him. Luckily Herrmann doesn't play cards; he only plays *with* them.

In the class of 1874 at Görlitz High School, there was no student less gifted than Fritz Herrmann. He didn't bring his report card home but instead took it across the border to Austria, to a tiny traveling circus, where he found a job as a poster painter. The boy learned how to do gymnastics on the ground and in the air, although he was really no good at it. At the age of sixteen, he went to Vienna and became an apprentice for Kratky Baschik. Anyone who knows the Prater in Vienna is aware that a booth bearing Kratky Baschik's name still exists today. Herrmann learned a great deal from his mentor and received thirty kreuzers for his presentation; that is, he was promised that amount but wound up getting five. Baschik had a problem with his lungs and had to stop one day, and Herrmann filled in for him.

He had always been a good speaker, and from observing chubby Baschik's techniques, he had become a more adept magician than his mentor. Both masters and servants gave him enthusiastic applause, his success grew, a good-sized audience turned up, and one day, so did Herr Rosenbaum, who hired Herrmann for the newly constructed "Venice in Vienna" at fifty guldens an evening.

High society was in attendance evening after evening, and Herrmann made a name for himself. He was even invited to the Sacher Hotel, where some gentlemen wished to have a private performance. Herrmann went there with three sparrows in his left pocket, which he had been carrying for months. He had gathered them up on Hauptallee when they were half-starved and trained them with a precise regimen, so they would fly away and come back when he whistled. The people here seemed quite refined. One of them pointed to a plate with three roasted fieldfares and said, "If you can bring them back to life, I'll give you my gold watch!" Herrmann put a fieldfare in his hand and deftly switched it for a sparrow, which fluttered up. Life came to the two other birds in the same manner. Herrmann was given the watch, and, because he had entertained the gentlemen so pleasingly, he also got a thousand guldens. As he then learned from the waiter, the man with the watch was King Milan of Serbia, the other gentlemen were Baron Rothschild, Baron Springer, Archduke Ferdinand, and Archduke Este.

Once he was in such fine company, Herrmann was not about to leave it. He spent forty years traveling back and forth throughout the world, always offering top-notch entertainment for the top people. He stayed at the sultan's court in Constantinople for seven years. He accepted an assignment from the shipowner Ballin to travel to America and back a dozen times to zero in on a card shark who was taking all the money away from the American passengers in poker, and nobody could discover his trick. Herrmann, too, needed twelve trips to figure it out: the man, an Austrian officer, always kept a gold snuffbox in front of him during the games. The snuffbox was matte on one side and glossy on the other. When this officer dealt the cards, he held the deck over the glossy side and thus knew his partners' cards: if he didn't see the joker in the deck, he pulled it out of his sleeve, as he had prepared for this express purpose. Herrmann put a stop to the amiable man's game.

Now seventy years old, he is indisputably the greatest card magician in the world. He turns down any offers to work in variety shows. He does perform, but only at private gatherings, whose hosts can offer him a thousand marks for two or three hours of work. At the moment, for example, he's packing his bags and traveling to Monte Carlo, where he has two sold-out evenings in the casino. The Monte Carlo shysters' eyeballs will be popping out of their heads, unable to catch on to even a single trick, let alone do the tricks themselves. Then Herrmann will be a guest at the German Club in Paris, and the following day the featured attraction at the home of a banking tycoon, whose guests he'll baffle so thoroughly that they won't be able to sleep for two weeks. The French ambassador won't win a single one of the hundred games of écarté, the American consul will lose the poker game with four of a kind. For the ladies of the house the ever-so-suave Herrmann will produce the ace of clubs for the jack of hearts, and he will guess which card they thought of without even touching the deck. All this comes off with an elegance not seen among card sharks, for Herrmann is more than that. He is a phenomenon on a par with Rafael Schermann.

Der Querschnitt, issue 6, June 1929

"Hello, Mr. Menjou?"

HE SPEAKS A CHARMING GERMAN—HIS MOTHER IS FROM LEIPZIG

W. R. Wilkerson drinks Coca-Cola: Coca-Cola, which tastes like burned tires. But it is said to be very refreshing. W. R. Wilkerson is in love with Coca-Cola. He is now on his fourth glass. When someone is in love with Coca-Cola, you can bet your last pair of pants, with wonderful odds, that this fan is an American. And if he pours four glasses into himself at once, he is surely a tired American.

W. R. Wilkerson is an American and he's tired. His card reads *Hollywood—New York*. He came with the S.S. *Bremen*; he didn't sleep in his quest to set new records.

W. R. Wilkerson wants to set up business in Berlin. In Hollywood he publishes a film newspaper dedicated to the actor Adolphe Menjou. He follows him to Europe, hoping to make films with him here, now that Menjou has fallen out with Paramount. One hundred thousand dollars for a film; that'll be the day. Adolphe had no intention of continuing to put up with this ridiculous price. No, he'd rather go fishing. He demands 150,000 dollars. Paramount doesn't go for that. The contract falls through. All of a sudden Menjou is overwhelmed by a mighty desire for Europe, no, for *work* in Europe. He packs his world-famous clothes into eighteen steamer trunks and is now in Paris. Meanwhile, Wilkerson is sounding out the situation in Berlin.

They want to start as soon as possible.

W. R. Wilkerson drinks another Coca-Cola. Awful, how can you have so many burned tires—. He looks at the clock. "Time to pay. Unfortunately I have to get to the office. A long-distance call with the Majestic Hotel, Paris, is coming. Would you like to make Menjou's acquaintance by telephone? Fine by me. I'll tell you everything as we go."

·

As we go he does indeed tell me everything.

One summer's day in 1919, a man in a light-gray suit crosses Hollywood Boulevard, a briefcase under his arm. On this day many men cross Hollywood Boulevard, many in light-gray suits and with briefcases under their arms, but none of them carry their briefcases the way our man does; no one walks in as focused a manner and yet as upright. That was striking, to us and to others. A car stops in front of the man.

"Pardon me. My name is Fairbanks. Douglas Fairbanks . . ." The man with the briefcase doffs his hat with magnificent elegance.

"Pleased to meet you. Adolphe Menjou."

Fifteen minutes later they're sitting across from each other at the studio.

"I'd like you to work for me!"

Menjou twirls the left end of his mustache. "I'm terribly sorry. I'm quite satisfied with my job as an agent for the C. C. Burr Enterprises film company. I earn 125 dollars a week, as well as percentages, plus a good Christmas bonus . . . for I am the best salesman in the place. And who can guarantee, Mr. Fairbanks, that I would distribute your films as well as I do our trash?"

"You wouldn't sell my films. You would act with me!"

Menjou now twirls the other end of his mustache. He signs the contract and thinks to himself: *insane.*

"Surely you are French, surely from a fine noble family?"

Menjou is delighted that he has already signed the contract. "Noble? My father is French, my mother is German, from Leipzig. I'm an American. Born in 1892. I was a waiter in my father's restaurant in Pittsburgh. Then I went to Cornell University, Ithaca, New York. In the war I served in France at the front. Then I was a motion picture agent. Until ten minutes ago I was still a salesman at C. C. Burr Enterprises. Now I'm the actor Adolphe Menjou. My brother will die laughing. And what, may I ask, will be my first role?"

"One of the Three Musketeers!"

One of the Three Musketeers catches Chaplin's eye. He signs him on and directs the film *A Woman of Paris: A Drama of Fate* (1923) with him and Purviance. Since then, Menjou's brother isn't dying of laughter anymore. Adolphe takes the ladder of success by storm, leaping up six rungs at a time. Lubitsch's *The Marriage Circle* (1924) already shows him in top form, then he is a room waiter for the grand duchess, the gentleman of Paris. He is considered the world's best-dressed man, along with the Prince of Wales, as the man with the two hundred suits and a thousand ties. His mustache, which had been the optical hallmark of the movie villain, sprouts offshoots on millions of upper lips, in America and Europe. He is one of the dozen people who can wear a tailcoat and a top hat, who can present a bouquet of flowers to a lady without occasioning a burst of laughter. Surely 100,000 per film was a bargain price for qualities like those.

When the contract ran out and Menjou wanted 150,000, Paramount didn't sign, ignoring the fact that it was letting go its last, its only true gentleman, someone with both poise and a fine voice, someone who would bring his sound film, *Fashions in Love* (1929), adapted from Hermann Bahr's play *Concert*, a great deal of success. Paramount does not give 150,000. Menjou is now in Paris. One cable after the other arrives. Their offer goes up to 125,000. Menjou doesn't budge. He simply makes two sound films with W. R. Wilkerson in Europe on his own. He's already working on two manuscripts with the author Ernst Bajda and will probably get the exquisite d'Abbadie d'Arrant as director. He doesn't yet know where he will shoot it, in London, in Paris, or in Berlin.

"Frankly, Berlin would be my preference!" says W. R. Wilk-erson. At this moment the long-distance office reports that Paris is on the line.

•

W. R. Wilkerson has put his feet up on the desk and is talking on the telephone with Adolphe Menjou, currently in Paris, Hotel Majestic. What I (a) can reveal, (b) have understood of Wilkerson's garbled American English is this: that he had seri-ous preliminary discussions with gentlemen from the German film industry on the *Bremen*; that he is going to Karlsbad today to see Laemmle to buy a story that Universal owns for Menjou; that he wants to begin production no later than October.

Then W. R. Wilkerson hands me the receiver. I don't know why, but at this moment I take a deep bow before Menjou, who is more than a thousand miles away, adjust my wretched tie pro-vocatively with my left hand. . . . Menjou speaks a very distinct and dignified German. Yes, he is looking forward to Berlin, quite a bit. Then he laughs when I state that Leipzig has ac-complished something besides the trade fair after all. No, he's traveling to Biarritz first to finish the scripts there. Work in Ber-lin? The odds are sixty to a hundred. It's all very nice and po-lite. At the end W. R. Wilkerson hollers a cheerful *goodbye* into the mouthpiece.

A damned invention. One sits in an office in Berlin, holds a silly receiver in one's hand, and sees the apartment in the Ma-jestic quite clearly: Adolphe sitting in front of the machine in silk pajamas, woven in Siam, changing his clothes for the fourth time. The ends of his mustache are now being drizzled with holy oil by a Japanese servant. Miss Kathryn Carver, his wife, is standing next to him and hasn't a clue what to do with the two hundred suits. Downstairs, on the set, six girls have been wait-ing for hours: they are bringing woolen ties they knitted for their Adolphe. But in the study, the elevator boy, who has the day off, is placing his autograph under a hundred photos: *Adolphe Menjou, Adolphe Menjou, Adolphe Menjou.*

Tempo, August 5, 1929

Klabund Died a Year Ago

THE WRITER AND THE DANCER FOR HIRE

That was a happy time, the winter of '26: back then I was a dancer for hire in a big hotel in Berlin.

Waiter no. 4, with whom I enjoyed a close friendship, had actually warned me about the table next to the banjo. All he had to do was give me a sidelong scowl as he walked by, and I knew instantly: you're not going to get a penny out of them. Oh, God, it didn't look as though a tip was forthcoming, either. Next to a charming woman a thin young man was sitting, gazing sadly and shyly at the dance floor and then up at the lights, which now turned a soft red. Soft red meant tango, and the dancing really is much better and much sweeter with this lighting. Yes, but better and sweeter didn't matter to me in the slightest back then. The weight, that was the question, whether one had to haul along 200 or just 180.

The Spaniards were just beginning to squeeze a sweet bit of music from their harmonicas. I wanted to duck out and give my legs a little breather, the wife of the distinguished financier having already trampled all over my sources of income during the foxtrot. But the dance instructor, a Russian who did not treat us well, caught me: the treadmill must not stand still for even a moment. So I went to this table, on the left next to the banjo, bowed in front of the sad young man, and began to sashay across the floor with his lady to a tango. While dancers for hire usually think about golden cigarette cases or new tie patterns while they dance, out of pure boredom, this lady was light on her feet and danced well. Every time we twirled past her young man, I watched him: he looked like Zinnemann.

Zinnemann had been the top student in our class, and we regularly copied our math homework from him. Terribly pale and thin, his hair cut short like a convict's. Poor Zinnemann— we had thought he would one day invent a perpetual-motion machine—had a problem with his lungs. They've long since buried him. Next to the young man I saw a cap lying on the chair, along with a couple of books. You'd be far more likely to find a cap at a five o'clock tea than books like these. . . . surely no book was ever seen again in this dance club.

They came back often. I danced with the lady, and the young man watched us quite jealously. Once, when I was standing around in the hall, he came right up to me. I was already fearing that he wanted to offer me a tip: what the devil, I would have been loath to take it from him.

"Pardon me . . ." he addressed me timidly, "I wanted to ask you . . . so a dancer for hire . . . that must be very interesting . . . I'd think, very interesting . . ."

"Nope, it's not."

His eyes looked back at me feverishly from behind his glasses. "No, really . . . excuse me for asking . . . but how do you get to be one?"

Funny thing; dancers for hire are always asked how you get to be one. To the ladies I danced with or who were learning to dance the Charleston for seven marks fifty, I always spun all sorts of tales, from "I've seen better days" and "family feud, disinheritance, getting away from it all," to "actually I wanted to become an aircraft designer," and "not all hope is lost quite yet." Still, I couldn't feed a pack of lies to this pale fellow, who looked

like my dead classmate Zinnemann: what can you do if you're
in bad shape? If your collar and cuffs can be reversed only twice?
If you can't spend the night on a bench in the Tiergarten during the winter? If the only line of credit you have is with a wine
merchant who added three bottles of Malaga to your tab, then
dumped this Malaga into the Landwehrkanal just to sell the
empty bottles.—Rolls cost money. What can you do?

He found that terribly interesting. "How about writing that
down, the way you told it to me. I'll place it in a newspaper!"
Yes, write . . . I had once done something along those lines, but
I wanted to try it again.

"So come to me; I'll help you!" He told me his address, near
Ernst-Reuter-Platz.

"Whom should I ask for?"

"Ask for Klabund."

*

On the following few days, the dance teacher was nowhere to
be seen in Grunewald. The Russian dance instructor was spit-
ting nails. I simply no longer showed up. At home I spent three
nights writing about what my legs had experienced. Then I
brought all of it to Klabund [aka Alfred Henschke]. He lived
with his wife, Carola Neher, the lady with whom I had danced
the tango.

My memoirs struck me as quite pathetic, but Klabund was
pleased, and sat there for an hour doing revisions. It occurred
to me to wonder what he might be doing to my text. Now and
then Klabund told me about having done something similar as
a piano player in a bar.

*

The *B. Z.* published my memoirs of a dancer for hire. But be-
forehand, Klabund wrote me a couple of lines of introduction.

We got together in a café, where he gave me these lines to use as a preface for the essays. Very fine words about how one should write about life as it is, and this was the way to go about it.

As we sat there, on that gray winter's morning, he looked even thinner, even paler. He held a handkerchief in front of his sunken mouth and coughed. "It's nothing," he said, and it really was nothing but a tiny red dot.

That is what he died of.

Tempo, August 12, 1929

III

Film and Theater Reviews

As a means of engaging with the contemporary film and theater scene, and to earn a little rent money in the process, Wilder wrote dozens of reviews and short accounts of studio and industry developments. He attended movie premieres and theater openings, covered the latest hits and flops, and wrote about most of these productions within the restricted space of a capsule review. His reviews cover the final phase of the silent era and the advent of sound, using the new Tri-Ergon sound-on-film technology, which came comparatively late to Germany. He notes the talent of the great silent stars Chaplin and Norma Shearer, of the newcomers Marlene Dietrich and Henny Porten, and also of the beloved down-market duo Ole and Axel (or "Pat und Patachon," as they were called in German). He offers a mixed review of Erich von Stroheim's epic *Greed* (1924) but has plenty of good things to say about the film industry of the late 1920s in general. In "First Silhouette Sound Film," Wilder writes admiringly of the pioneering animation work by Lotte Reiniger and its impact on *Fräulein Fähnrich* (*Miss Midshipman*, 1929), and his review of the American director Arthur Rosson's *The Winged Horseman* (1929) affords him the chance to wax rhapsodic about the filmic portrayals of the American West—the source of his own nickname and the cultural mythology that captured the hearts of scores of European filmgoers—churned out on the backlots of Hollywood studios.

Wilder's theater reviews feature a piece marking the fiftieth performance of Bertolt Brecht's megahit *Threepenny Opera*, extolling the virtues of Kurt Weill's music as well as the supreme acting of cabaret greats Rosa Valetti and Kurt Gerron, and a somewhat skeptical piece on John van Druten's *Young Woodley* at Berlin's Deutsches Theater. Although Wilder never showed much interest in Zionism elsewhere, in his review of *Springtime in Palestine*, an oddly compelling documentary of 1928 by Josef Gal-Ezer, he exhibits a degree of genuine curiosity, even sympathy. "We see European girls from bourgeois families who did office work or studied at universities back home now building streets," he writes, "men previously unaccustomed to agrarian life now cultivating the soil." He closed by noting that the applause in the theater was noticeably enthusiastic, something he himself would strive for, and nearly always achieve, in his own subsequent work as a writer-director.

Broken Barriers (1924)

A NEW SHEARER-MENJOU FILM

A film like a hundred other American ones; the interesting part is the subject matter, which is amazingly liberal; also of interest are four outstanding actors: Norma Shearer, James Kirkwood, Adolphe Menjou, Mae Bush.

The subject: Ward Trenton, who has been separated from his wife for years, is a misogynist, until Grace, a saleswoman, the youngest member of the impoverished Durland family, comes his way, in the following manner: Tommy Kemp, a friend of Irene and Gerti's co-worker, organizes an orgy. Trenton is also there, and he makes sure Grace gets home before the explosion. Grace is in love with Ward Trenton. She (an American girl from a good family!) wants to break down the barriers imposed by morality and conventions and devote herself unconditionally to Trenton.

Meanwhile, Ward's wife comes back, and the three—Grace, Ward, and Ward's wife—happen to meet up at the home of Frau Reynolds; ugly scenes ensue: Frau Trenton will not hear of a divorce and insults Grace, who, in order to prevent a scandal, leaves the party. Now Grace knows she can never become Ward's wife. And she wants to belong to Trenton more fervently than ever.

Ward struggles with himself, and goodness wins out. Grace now sees Ward less often. But one night, four old friends take part in a car trip: Grace, Mr. Durland, Irene, Ward Trenton, and—at the steering wheel—Tom Camp, dead drunk. The car drives through a forest at breakneck speed and flips over; the four of them have an accident. Tom Camp dies in Irene's arms, Grace recovers quickly, Ward Trenton winds up in the hospital. There the physician sets up a little trap; he leads Trenton's wife to believe that Ward will always remain a cripple. Then she demands a divorce from him and moves out. Now Grace can marry Trenton, who has a full recovery.

The cast: Grace Durland is played by Norma Shearer, a very personable young actress, beautiful, good figure, talented. Mae Bush, an outstanding actress who unfortunately receives too little attention, plays Irene. James Kirkwood does a solid job as Ward Trenton, playing him as serious and aristocratic, fully aware that his role entails embodying a Yankee imbued with the morality and conventions of America.

And then there is Adolphe Menjou (Tommy Kemp). His is only a supporting role, but it is brilliantly acted, full of inspiration and spicy details. Menjou, discovered by Chaplin and launched by Lubitsch, is today one of the most appealing and ingenious figures in American film.

Die Bühne, April 8, 1926

Ehekonflikte (Marital Conflicts, 1927)

AT THE PRIMUS PALACE

A wife is surprised by her husband while in her boudoir with another man. She pretends that she was attacked and that he is the burglar. But as the police are about to take him away, she reveals the hoax. She travels to Nice, the other man travels to Nice, the husband travels to Nice, and all three take up residence in the same hotel. And here the ludicrous game with the superficial conflicts continues, with the theft of a secret treaty added in for good measure, until the other man—who is the document thief—brings the married couple back together.

The writing, by Erich Herzog, and direction, by Alfons Berthier, are unbelievably clumsy. The second half was greeted with more and more laughter and whistles, and when the title card "These were awful hours" appeared toward the end, the audience chimed in with uproarious approval. Too bad that Lotte Lorring, Werner Pitschau, and Victor Colani were willing to stoop to this level for "baloney," as the author sees it.

It was preceded by an equally weak American adventure film, *Menschen der Nacht* (*Men of the Night*, 1926).

B. Z. am Mittag, June 3, 1927

Eichberg Shoots a Film

When Richard Eichberg shoots a film, fun is sure to follow, and so the large studio set in Neubabelsberg is now reverberating with merry music. *Der Fürst von Pappenheim* (*The Masked Mannequin*, 1927), adapted from the well-known opera, is designed to set just the right mood. Egon Fürst, who manages fashion models, and his alter ego, "Fürst Egon," are played by Curt Bois, and Mona Maris, an actress newly discovered by Eichberg, has the role of Princess Antoinette. The cast also features Dina Gralla and Werner Fütterer. The cinematography is by Heinrich Gärtner.

G. W. Pabst, the director of *Die Liebe der Jeanne Ney* (*The Love of Jeanne Ney*, 1927), has spent hours standing outdoors in the searing sun, waiting for rain. And he succeeds in compelling the heavens to provide a downpour with lightning and thunder. The result is quite a soggy treat, and the scene is "true to life." Now Pabst has gone to Paris with his lead actors and actresses, Brigitte Helm, Edith Jehanne, Uno Henning, and Fritz Rasp, and cameramen Fritz Arno Wagner and Walter Robert Lach, to film the outdoor scenes.

On a different part of the set, Dr. Fritz Wendhausen is working on the final shots for his film *Der Kampf des Donald Westhofs* (*The Trial of Donald Westhof*, 1927), adapted from the novel in the Berlin newspaper *Illustrirte Zeitung*. A scene in Spiess's saloon, with a characteristic view onto the street, looks so natural that viewers think they are seeing the home turf of Elizza La Porta, Imre Ráday, Nicolai Malikoff, and Hermann Vallentin.

B. Z. am Mittag, June 7, 1927

Der Bettler vom Kölner Dom (*The Beggar from Cologne Cathedral*, 1927)

This rousing, fast-paced detective film provides good entertainment because it's fun. Dr. Alfieri's screenplay draws on a tried-and-true model, pitting a gang of thieves—who adopt many guises in their attempts to rob a young lady's jewelry—against a famous detective, and he has a knack for tying together and tying up situations and imbuing the overall plot with a gentle, sometimes glitzy humor that nicely tones down the tension.

The shot sequences of the director, Rolf Randolf, move along rapidly and thus effectively. The acting is also very good. Harry Lamberz-Pausen, spiffed up as a "dashing fellow," using his athletic strength to break into a strongbox, reels in hearty laughter. Henry Stuart plays the detective with genteel reserve, and Hanni Weisse, Fritz Kampers, Karl de Vogt, and Robert Scholz make for well-conceived characters as the band of thieves. The sets by G. A. Knauer and Willie Hameister's camera work are quite lovely.

B. Z. am Mittag, August 30, 1927

Pat und Patachon am Nordseestrand (*Ole and Axel at the North Sea Shore*, 1927)

AT THE EMELKA PALACE

Seeing old friends after a long time is always a pleasure. And it was nice to see these two wacky, funny fellows, tall, skinny Ole and short, chubby Axel, who were coming from the North Sea shore, where they had experienced all kinds of things. The tales they told call to mind Münchhausen's fanciful stories. They gave fishing a try but came to realize that they themselves could easily wind up being fished by a shark. They built a cabin, which the wind blew away one night, while they themselves wound up buried in the sand (inspired by a scene in Chaplin's *The Gold Rush*). They were heroes, of course. Axel, undaunted even by ghosts, was the greater of the two. They won the hearts of the village beauties with their droll way of dancing the Charleston, freed a young man from the hands of his rival, and helped him find a way to marry the woman he loves.

These are amusing Don Quixote–style capers, harmless, goofy, executed with unflappable poise and hence amusing. Lau Lauritzen produced lovely outdoor shots and, in the scene where the castaways are rescued, created some suspense as well. It was a lovely evening.

B. Z. am Mittag, September 9, 1927

Funkzauber (Radio Magic, 1927)

AT THE PHOEBUS PALACE

For fans of radio—and there are quite a few of those!—this film has much to offer. It guides them through the broadcast studios in Berlin, acquaints them with the announcers on the major stations, especially with the much-admired Berlin announcer Alfred Braun, and gives them an instructive picture of the workings of broadcasting, affording them hours of the liveliest entertainment from a magical distance—not in dry images but in the framework of an appealing storyline by Jane Bess and Dr. Rino Ottavi, directed by Richard Oswald, overly sweeping in scope but still lively.

This film, with a humorous touch, is about a radio enthusiast who settles in for some serious listening without paying for the privilege wherever he goes, whether it be in the woods, as he happily munches on his sandwich, or at the police station, where he is brought in as a vagrant, or in his shack, to which his dream of inheriting a million has shrunk. Werner Krauss endows this character with an impeccable and easygoing humor. This radio devotee, his hat askew and a twinkle in his eye, is a peppy fellow. Krauss's performance in this film is on a par with his magnificent portrayal of a petty official in *A Royal Scandal*.

Besides him, the actors are not very memorable: Xenia Desni, who once again has to play the role of a young girl, Fern Andra, is a welcome presence, and it would be nice to see her more often in roles that offer her more to work with; Leo Penkdert as a well-educated man who is a foe of radio and thus enraged; Anton Pointner as a slick scoundrel; Fritz Kampers as a policeman; and Gert Briese as a soulful lover. There was abundant applause from the audience.

B. Z. am Mittag, October 4, 1927

Frost in the Studio

A BATH AT TWENTY DEGREES FAHRENHEIT

Film actors certainly have it hard at times! One example could be seen recently at the studio in Staaken, where the French director Jacques Feyder is shooting the film *Thérèse Raquin* for the Defu. On the set is a tumbledown country inn with a giant pool, a "lake" in which the unfaithful Thérèse and her lover drown her feeble husband. In the summer, the actors would surely have welcomed a water scene of this sort. But they are to be admired for not losing their composure and willingly and eagerly carrying out the scene, with teeth chattering, at the cold temperature of twenty degrees Fahrenheit. Gina Manés, Wolfgang Zilzer, and A. H. Schlettow are this gutsy trio.

The Defu is at the same time filming *Seine Mutter* [aka *Ehre Deine Mutter*] (*Honor Thy Mother*, 1928), directed by Paul Ludwig Stein. The American actress Mary Carr plays the leading role. Then there is *Frau Sorge* (*Dame Care*, 1928), directed by Robert Land, which stars Mary Carr as well. Dieterle and Grete Mosheim are also leading cast members.

B. Z. am Mittag, November 29, 1927

Ole and Axel at Beba Palace

"On the Path to Strength and Beauty" completes the film's title. And they might have added, "and to two lovely wives," because these two schlemiels, who so often lose their hearts to creatures with skinny legs but always have to resignedly watch others be chosen in their place, are now able to come out ahead of two sweet and somewhat asinine young men.

But the tall skinny one and the short chubby one come in handy for many things. There are two jolly girls who have been fleecing their uncle in the country under the pretense of studying painting and sculpture in the city, and when the uncle decides to drop in to visit his nieces, the two men play along with a plan to pose as Roman and Greek statues. Then they act as a droll pair of teachers in a dance and gymnastics school that the girls set up in their uncle's country home. Paying them with love is the least the girls can do.

The plot is very amusing. Ole and Axel wind up in any number of tricky situations and always find a delightful way out. Lau Lauritzen, their standard director, staged this film with humor and a good deal of verve, thus providing quite a fun evening, received with hearty applause.

B. Z. am Mittag March 9, 1928

Der Geliebte seiner Frau (*His Wife's Lover*, 1928)

AT THE MARMORHAUS

The subtitle, "A Fling into the Marriage Bed," holds out the promise of a bawdy, funny film. But the authors, Fritz Zoreff and Siegfried Berenfeld, have diluted their wine with quite a bit of water. To their credit, they refrained from any coarseness, but they did not come up with the light touch and liveliness that would have made this overused subject matter worth seeing one more time in a silly little comedy.

The story—of the commoner's daughter and the impoverished count who are supposed to marry to get him out of debt and get her the count's coronet she longs for but who fall in love before the wedding without realizing who their partner actually is—is not a new one. But there's too much squeezed in here. We've seen these motifs and situations in far more pleasing and appealing forms. Max Neufeld's role as director lacks pacing and subtle nuances. Dina Gralla is not shown off to best advantage in the leading role, and her acting is uncertain. Her partner, Alfons Fryland, is equally weak. Claire Lotta tries and utterly fails to infuse her role with any spirit. Richard Waldemar, however, does breathe life into the role of a delightful old charmer.

B. Z. am Mittag, March 30, 1928

From the Studios

Out in St. Pauli, a disreputable part of Hamburg, is "The Good Anchorage" bar. The sailors who hang out there are not exactly the best. The two really bad guys are "The Nipper" (Wolfgang Zilzer) and "The Doctor" (Fritz Rasp), to whom the most beautiful girl in St. Pauli (Jenny Jugo) lures victims so they can be robbed. She is known as the "Carmen of St. Pauli," a name that gave the title to the film (*Docks of Hamburg*, 1928) Erich Waschnek is now shooting in Neubabelsberg with cinematographer Friedel Behn-Grund and set designer Alfred Junge. A good and honest sailor (Willy Fritsch), who happens into this sort of bar for the first time, also winds up in her clutches. These people! We're secretly glad that we're only meeting up with them in a faithfully replicated St. Pauli.

The film *Karneval der Liebe* (*Love's Masquerade*, 1928), on which Augusto Genina is working, takes us into a different milieu, friendly, light, and fun-filled.

B. Z. am Mittag, May 8, 1928

Greed (1924)

AT THE KAMERA

This small repertory theater, on Unter den Linden, which has already brought new glory to many an old film, has now become the advocate for this Stroheim film, which had to be canceled abruptly after its premiere in Berlin. There are no more signs of the outrage that erupted back then over this cruelly naturalistic depiction of the depths to which humans can sink.

But it is depressing to watch this depiction of the human condition, which consistently brings the flip side of more accustomed outcomes to the screen, yet it is also lopsided and full of meaningless symbols. Still, parts of it paint a stirring portrait of the soul of a woman whose greed arouses all her baser impulses, and the poignancy of the acting also makes it gripping. Seeing this film is not relaxing, but it is still a pleasure, though different from the usual kind.

B. Z. am Mittag, July 10, 1928

A Blonde for a Night (1928)

AT THE SCHAUBURG

It is hard to tell what the title of this film has to do with the transformation of a confirmed bachelor and misogynist into the most respectable husband. During these dog days the film could certainly seem enticing. You'd almost be sorry to get caught up—unwittingly—in this silly set of circumstances if the film weren't made in such a buoyant and humorous manner. Marie

Prevost deploys all her charm and bubbly nature, Franklin Pangborn his dry humor, and Harrison E. Ford his great acting to offer light and pleasant entertainment.

B. Z. am Mittag, July 17, 1928

The Valley of the Giants (1927)

AT THE SCHAUBURG

Splendid, these gigantic, thousand-year-old redwood trees, near whose mighty trunks people look like Lilliputians, splendid, these primeval forest landscapes, in which weather-beaten people perform their strenuous daily tasks. They form a superb backdrop for a story—and unfortunately an all-too-American one—of two dogged rivals in the lumber industry.

We don't understand these unwritten laws in which the fist rules. But there are several scenes, such as the swift descent, that are gripping, and in parts there are welcome injections of humor that provide a break from the near-constant nasty fighting. Enjoyable actors, Milton Sills and Doris Kenyon, ably assist the director, Charles J. Brabin, in presenting an unfamiliar but interesting milieu.

B. Z. am Mittag, July 27, 1928

Die grosse Liebe (*The Last Night,* 1928)

The Jacobins are camping in the Tronville castle hotel. These tough, grim men form into groups on bits of straw. Between them are pyramids of weapons, with large cooking pots hanging down. The fire slowly dies out. Some of the soldiers are already awake, enjoying themselves while splashing on some water at the castle well. Then the whole group comes alive. Three horsemen burst through the castle gate. Their leader delivers an important message to the officer. On they gallop, while back in the courtyard commands are shouted out, short and sharp—the day will begin with a bloody tribunal. A traitor in front of a tribunal.

An exceedingly picturesque scene from the Terra-Film *The Last Night*, which is now being shot on the grounds and in the Terra-Glashaus. The script is by Norbert Falk and Robert Liebmann; the director is A. W. Sandberg. In the leading roles are Fritz Kortner, Gösta Ekman, Diomira Jacobini, Karina Bell, and Walter Rilla.

B. Z. am Mittag, July 31, 1928

In the Name of the Law (1922)

AT THE PRIMUS PALACE

The navy, the army, the air force, and now also the police, everything that represents state power over the public and embodies it, is held up high in American films of late. If this film had not aspired to be more than a detective story, it would have had enough elements of suspense to captivate viewers. But a mawkish story about an elderly policeman was tacked on, the inanity of which spoils things and doesn't even let the suspense added on toward the end work its magic.

Emory Johnson's direction veers off into a series of subplots that go off on tangents, and it eventually loses the necessary momentum in portraying the battle of the police, represented by the aging policeman and his son, who is a police pilot, against a gang of jewel thieves. On a technical level, the film is a disappointment. And the airplane pursuit of the ringleader of the gang makes us painfully aware of its makeshift studio work. The final battle at the jeweler's lacks the kind of bone-chilling escalation you expect from American suspense films, even though there are explosions, fires, and a great number of firemen at work. The acting is on this same level.

B. Z. am Mittag, August 3, 1928

Sounds Are Recorded

THE STUDIO SHOTS

Imagine you've been invited to be a guest at a house and you show up on time but find the doors locked. That's what happened to me recently when I visited a studio. A servant stands in front of the door yet doesn't open it for the visitor; instead, he holds it firmly locked and keeps a good eye on it, refusing to let anyone enter. Here's why—a talking picture is being filmed.

And now we know: sounds, words, and noises may be produced, spoken, and generated, but only when they are suitable for the scenes, whereas reverberating steps of arriving guests are unlikely to have been intended for the scene being shot. So we wait outside until there's a break.

Then we can watch Max Mack, who once made the first German *Autorenfilm*, a signature film of the era, now cranking out the first German sound film using the Tri-Ergon system, silently directing his actors with miming movements of his head, hands, and sometimes his feet, as long as it's not with his mouth.

"Crank" is not really the right expression, because the camera, four times as large as the usual camera used for films, doesn't actually have a crank. Once it is adjusted and everything is ready for the shoot, the cameraman activates it by means of an electrical contact, and automatically the camera records the images and sounds on a rolling celluloid tape in parallel strips—incorporating the sounds by electrically converting sound waves into light oscillations—to make image and sound form a complete unit.

The volume is controlled and relayed by the amplifier, an equally complicated machine, which is electrically linked to the camera. The reigning king, Joseph Massolle, inventor of the Tri-Ergon system, is on-site, monitoring the sound design, which requires a comprehensive balancing of the acoustic conditions. For this purpose the room undergoes some degree of sound-proofing, because sound comes across differently on a big set than in a closed room.

Microphones are mounted, out of sight, wherever the actors will be standing at a given moment, to make sounds and gestures match up perfectly and coordinate with where the sounds are directed. The actor, who has to pay attention not only to his facial expressions but also to the text and the way the words are expressed, faces substantial difficulties that necessitate exhaustive rehearsals.

The plot of this first talking picture [*Ein Tag Film* (*A Day in Film*, 1928)], which is expected to be about five hundred yards long, was also created by Max Mack and offers many avenues to employ speech and other sounds. The viewer experiences all that goes on behind the scenes. A woman (Georgia Lind) who wishes to become an actress against the wishes of her husband (Kurt Vespermann) is instructed to play a scene and bungles it, then has repeated confrontations with the director (Paul Graetz) and production manager before conceding her ineptitude.

We will only know the extent to which the resistant acoustic material has been successfully integrated when dialogues, sounds on the set, and film music are shown in the finished product.

The advanced Tri-Ergon system, however, might well raise our hopes that we have moved ahead nicely in sound film.

B. Z. am Mittag, August 21, 1928

The Threepenny Opera, for the Fiftieth Time

At the Theater am Schiffbauerdamm, *The Threepenny Opera* has now reached its fiftieth performance. The opera's enduring appeal owes to its fusion of outrageous wit and social criticism. Kurt Weill's music is a large part of that appeal. The Beggar King is now played by Hans Hermann Schaufuss, and his daughter, Polly, is Charlotte Ander. Rosa Valetti is superb as "a woman tailor-made for procuring and for the Gypsy trade," whereas Harald Paulsen is a very likable murderer, robber, and swindler. Kate Kühl invariably gets extra applause for her brilliantly trenchant performance. Kurt Gerron lends tragicomic tenderness to the role of the sheriff of London, who takes kickbacks from that scoundrel Mackie. There was just as much applause for this fiftieth performance as there had been for the first.

B. Z. am Mittag, October 22, 1928

Frühling in Palästina / Aviv be'Erez Israel (Springtime in Palestine, 1928)

Twenty-five years ago a barren desert with noxious swamps, today a city with forty-five thousand residents, lovely wide streets, handsome garden villas, schools, sanatoriums, factories, the future seaside resort of the Orient—Tel Aviv. The second powerful impression is that of Haifa, the port city of Palestine, now being greatly expanded. The many communities appear before your eyes in vibrant images, extensive orange plantations, which already yield two million crates a year, the main export product, and there are fields and forests.

All wrested in hard, tedious work from the sandy, rocky soil. We see European girls from bourgeois families who did office work or studied at universities back home now building streets, men previously unaccustomed to agrarian life now cultivating the soil. Also of interest are the images from the interior of Palestine, of Jerusalem, the Dead Sea, the Sea of Galilee, the rapids of the Jordan River, which will now be used to generate electricity.

This film is a unique cultural document, a paean to willpower and work. Josef Gal-Ezer made it quite skillfully. The applause was enthusiastic.

B. Z. am Mittag, December 11, 1928

First Silhouette Sound Film

FRÄULEIN FÄHNRICH (MISS MIDSHIPMAN, 1929)

Who doesn't know the little [Julius] Pinschewer films, those amusing little animations that form the core of the preliminary program in many moving-picture theaters? Pinschewer has now gone a step further, and we've been following his experiment with great interest as we watch the results. The goal is to connect advertising films with sound films using the Tri-Ergon system.

The entertaining form Pinschewer chose drew on Lotte Reiniger's silhouette animations. It took him seven months to put together seventy thousand individual images to create a little film, 275 yards in length, loosely based on Andersen's *The Chinese Nightingale*. The contents amount to an advertisement for Tri-Ergon films. This type of filming continues to pose several technical difficulties, of course, in spite of good continuing development, and the text for the plot had to be supplied by the tinny voice of an announcer, because a dialogue simultaneous with the moving images could not be achieved. Even so, this and other tests show that there is still much to be accomplished in this arena.

The film *Fräulein Fähnrich* (*Miss Midshipman*, 1929), now playing at the Primus Palace, is meant to be a witty story about the navy. The three writers did not shy away from listing their names and claiming responsibility for the tritest absurdities in witless situations and situationless witticisms. The highest degree of goodwill: not a word about them and their crimes. You have to feel sorry for Mary Parker, Fritz Schulz, and the whole big crowd of extras who had to act so sweet and dopey, and for the audience that had to watch this.

B. Z. am Mittag, March 5, 1929

Was eine Frau im Frühling träumt (*What a Woman Dreams in Spring*, 1929)

AT THE BAVARIA LICHTSPIELE

What does a little shorthand typist dream of in the spring? Naturally, that's the kind of person this film is about, just like so many other recent films. And it's just as natural that a sudden windfall, beautiful clothing, the French Riviera town of Nice, an amorous adventure, and a famous film star add up to the sum of all hopes and dreams. If a few more painful cuts were to be made, a nice film would result—or so Hans Bietzke and Curt Blachnitzky thought. But the events and emotions they picked up from the hit song by Walter Kollo are unoriginal and not told well enough to arouse more interest.

On top of that, Blachnitzky's directing lacks rhythm. The whole thing could use a bit of sun, of spring. Colette Brettel looks quite nice but suffers from the lifelessness of the direction, as does Ernst Rückert, the movie enthusiast in the film. Kurt Vespermann and Julius Falkenstein provide some amusement.

B. Z., April 2, 1929

"Youth Stage"?

I wonder whether the youngsters, the drama students at the Deutsches Theater, had a part in choosing the play that was presented yesterday on the rehearsal stage of the Kammerspiele. I hope not! This play, *Young Woodley*, by John van Druten, employs his boyish charm, sentimental sparkle, and the pure folly of his marvelously youthful mentality, but in essence it is undermined by his know-it-all attitude and precocious panache. Even so, it is deftly constructed, with slick dialogue, and some of its clever lines attest to meticulous craftsmanship.

It's about the old, yet eternally new, story of how a nice boy who is not predestined to tragedy nearly stumbles into a life-threatening situation when he takes his first steps into the seemingly paradisiacal existence of adults. If only Young Woodley . . . ! [. . .] the play would have been much more pleasant than one depicting a quick conversion to resigned middle-class life. Hans-Joachim Moebis in the title role,

Franziska Benthoi as his idol, and Gustav Specht as an up-and-coming young comedian could develop into actors if they stay in good hands.

B. Z., May 18, 1929

Stroll through the Studios—
They're Shooting Silent Films

Sprengbagger at the Terra-Glashaus

Dr. [Carl Ludwig] Achaz-Duisberg calls his new film *Sprengbagger 1010*, and he's shot it himself—his first time doing so. Hans von Wolzogen assisted as production manager, and [Artur] von Schwertführer as cameraman. The destruction of the earth by the expansion of industry forms the basis of the film. The actual plot, which is designed to sell tickets, features popular actors, the lovely Viola Garden and Ilse Stobrava first and foremost, as well as Heinrich George and [Ivan] Koval-Samborsky.

Marlene Dietrich's Night Flight

At the airfield in Staaken is a plane that is wide, gray, and massive—illuminated in violet by the beacon lights. The wing and fuselage bear the number D 1231. So this is no ordinary airplane—it is the plane that has set a record by remaining in the air for sixty-five hours.

What's it doing here at the Staaken airfield? It's part of a film plot—in the Max Glass Film production company's moving picture that is shooting *Schiff der verlorenen Menschen* (*The Ship of Lost Men*, 1929)—and stops here when Marlene Dietrich sets out for the night flight that pulls her out of the ballroom, only to race her off to the isolation of the ocean: the night scene shows the departure, which keeps being rehearsed, again and again, then is finally filmed. Reliable, true, and without a hitch, the aircraft plays along . . . it likely knows that after setting a record a victor has to be filmed, so it undergoes that process with propriety and grace.

The New Henny Porten Film

A few months ago a strange case of a longing for motherhood drove a woman to steal someone else's child. Henny Porten read the report in the *B. Z.* and then could not let go of this subject and built on it. Friedrich Raff and Julius Urgiss wrote the script for the film, which she now shot with Georg Jacoby as the director. Her scenes, which were shown in Staaken, are stirring: simple, sincere, teary—real tears, her mouth trembling as if she's experiencing this herself, as her hands searchingly grasp the child, a surprisingly gifted child actress, that little Inge. The child's parents are played by Elisabeth Pinajeff and Ernst Stahl-Nachbaur.

Dieterle Is Once Again Making a Film

Wilhelm Dieterle, who seemed to have disappeared altogether from the stage and screen for quite a long time, can be seen in the studio again working on a new film. Using a screenplay by his wife, Charlotte Hagenbruch, he plays the leading role in *Frühlingsrauschen—Tränen, die ich dir geweint* (*Rustle of Spring—Tears I Shed for You*, 1929) with Lien Deyers, Vivian Gibson, and Elsa Wagner; Dieterle directed the film himself.

Experimental Films

Filmstudio 1929 was founded as the first German film studio under the leadership of Moriz Seeler, Robert Siodmak, and Edgar Ulmer. Filmstudio 1929 will make experimental films on a cooperative basis, independently of any industry requirements. The studio is launching its work with the film *Summer 29*. The cast consists entirely of nonactors.

The New Ufa Program, 1929–30

The new Ufa production comprises twenty lavish productions, most of which are being produced as Ufa sound films. The necessity arises to shoot completely independent silent versions for all the Ufa sound films; that is, hundreds of yards are shot for these films that are not incorporated into the sound film version, but have to be made in order to supply a first-class silent film to theaters that cannot play sound films. On the other hand, the silent films for the theaters that are equipped to show sound films get a sound film entertainment consisting of music, background noises, and sound effects.

The Richest Woman in the World

This French *Travel Adventure in Two Parts of the World* is a complete failure. You don't even get to enjoy the enticing Egyptian landscape and the ancient cultural monuments, because the photography is deeply flawed. It would be best to lay a veil of charitable silence over the contents, which are pure unadulterated kitsch. The directors (M. Bandal and Ch. Delac), who poured a great deal of tedious love into it, and Lee Parry—oh, don't get me started!

B. Z., June 21, 1929

Das verschwundene Testament (*The Missing Will*, 1929)

AT THE KAMMERSPIELE

When Carlo Aldini, a detective, is on a case, fighting on two fronts, the vagabonds in front of him and the police behind, there is sure to be tension, shockers. Pursuit, attack, escape, chase scene—wild adventures, which he handles with fabulous verve and astonishing acrobatic agility. A real man!

All Rolf Randolf, scriptwriter (with Dr. Emanuel Alfieri) and director, had to do was give Aldini the catchwords and put him into the right position. He did so exceedingly well. It offers peppy entertainment. There is also a healthy dose of humor with the delightful supporting character that Siegfried Arno plays to gripping comic effect. Daisy d'Ora is also quite nice. Hans Junkermann, Jack Mylong-Münz, and J. W. Speerger complete the animated ensemble. There was hearty applause.

B. Z., July 9, 1929

The Winged Horseman (1929)

AT THE UFA PAVILION

These stories from the Wild West, involving villainous caretakers, rapacious neighbors, and brutish highwaymen, are certainly rough-hewn, and the episodes are naïvely devised right down to the end, yet there is something impressive about these prairie films. When they are shot with as much experience and as much zest as Arthur Rosson has done here, their effect is disarming and rousing, particularly with a hotshot like the incomparably quick-witted Hoot Gibson in the lead role. And he also has a compelling sense of humor. Ruth Elder, the aviatrix, does not do badly at all in her introduction to film. There was hearty applause.

B. Z., August 13, 1929

Männer ohne Beruf (*Men without Work*, 1929)

AT THE UFA PALACE AM ZOO

Harry Piel goes after traffickers of girls! A multitalented fellow who makes mincemeat out of the bad guys, hounding them through the crooked alleys and hideouts of Marseille, and the result is great fun.

Robert Liebmann proves to be an excellent guide through the labyrinth of convoluted pathways of an interesting, gripping detective adventure rich in humorous incidents. And Harry, an accomplished actor, knows just how to set the scene for these kinds of things, with verve and wit, captivatingly and entertainingly.

As an actor, Piel [also the director] is as endearing as ever. Dary Holm, acting alongside him, is quite striking, and the large additional cast, most interesting among them the jovial Albert Paulig and the talented Edith Meinhard, works well in their supporting roles. The success was strong and genuine.

B. Z., August 14, 1929

Laubenkolonie [aka *Die lustigen Musikanten*] (*The Merry Musicians*, 1930)

AT THE PRIMUS PALACE

An amusing sound film. The milieu is Berlin, not always on the mark, but seen with humor and performed entertainingly. Franz Rauch and Max Obal, who also directed it with zest and gusto, have taken a clear-eyed look at community gardening plots and captured some charming encounters. A nice, unsentimental love story and an elderly widower's unpalatable excursion into a second marriage to a cabaret singer hold together the slightly divergent series of scenes.

The audience caught on well to the charming slapstick, and their amusement was enhanced by the actors' clear enthusiasm. Fritz Kampers once again plays a tough, stalwart country boy; Camilla Spira, who is seen in film far too infrequently, a sweet, likable girl. Hermann Picha and Erika Glässner, the mismatched married couple, and Julius Falkenstein and Hans Hermann Schaufuss add an element of humor, sometimes of their own creation when the scene didn't provide any.

B. Z., October 25, 1930

Susanne macht Ordnung (*Susie Cleans Up*, 1930)

AT THE ATRIUM

A farce, with a little singing, a little dancing, and a good bit of humor: contented faces, robust applause, a success that feels particularly fulfilling because there were two "first-timers" shown to fine advantage with this premiere. The writer-director, Eugen Thiele, and his co-author, Wolfgang Wilhelm, did not come up with a terribly original plot, but they enliven it with a refreshing, incisive situational comedy.

Thiele moves along at the rapid clip with which such inconsequential things, intended solely for entertainment, have to be filmed, and the cast follows him eagerly and enthusiastically. At the head is Szöke Szakall, attorney for extremely difficult cases, who has had an excellent day. In the same vein there is a set of unwitting fathers—Truus Van Aalten is on a very spirited quest—the humorous Kurt Lilien and Martin Kettner, while the real father, Albert Paulig, stays discreetly in the background, and Max Ehrlich's unflappable composure works nicely as he pulls the strings in a little game of intrigue. The role of lover is well served by Franz Lederer.

B. Z., November 21, 1930

Translator's Note

When Noah Isenberg approached me with a plan to bring together the early journalism of Billy Wilder, I couldn't say yes fast enough. Who doesn't love Billy Wilder? Surely we *all* like it hot, Wilder-style. Osgood Fielding III may have declared that "nobody's perfect," but Billy Wilder's filmmaking comes awfully close to perfection.

I'd never read Wilder's early journalism, but once Noah supplied me with the two books on which this compilation draws, all composed in the 1920s, I was entranced all over again by Wilder's powers of observation that shed light and laughter on the human condition. Wilder's "outsize gift of gab," as Noah aptly describes it, is in full evidence here. Wilder's humor is sly, subtle, and oblique, giving rise less to belly laughs than to ongoing chuckles.

Noah had already pored over the collections of Wilder's journalism, then I joined in the fun. What a cornucopia awaited us! We sought out a selection that would introduce readers to Wilder's reflections on current films, the latest cultural and fashion trends, fickle weather patterns, his own plans to shoot a film, and his encounters with celebrities—Ernst Lubitsch, Cornelius Vanderbilt, Asta Nielsen, Paul Whiteman, the Tiller Girls—as well as a host of quirky "ordinary people," such as the lucky (real or imagined) individual who earned his living by smiling uninterruptedly. Wilder's range is vast: we learn how the smell of matches has evolved, how efforts to modernize cafés wind up erasing our collective memories, how a business tycoon can't manage to see a dentist, how the Prince of Wales suffers from an absurdly privileged ennui, how the art of telling lies ought to figure in the school curriculum. . . . And we learn, in two pieces about Wilder's work as a dancer for hire, how that humble job opened the door to his pursuit of journalism.

His essays engage and quicken our senses, as Wilder's "eager nostrils" chase down scents or as he brings musical life to inanimate objects, such as in this passage from "Renovation, an Ode to the Coffeehouse," which infuses the atmosphere of a café with the tones of what Wilder calls the "molecular miracle" of "metaphysical ensoulment":

> Coffeehouses have something in common with well-played violins. They resonate, reverberate, and impart distinct timbres. The many years of the regular guests' clamor have stored their filaments and atoms in a singular way, and the woodwork, paneling, and even pieces of furniture pulse marvelously to the tunes of the visitors' life rhythms. Malice and venomous thoughts of a decade on the blackened walls have settled in as a sweetly radiant finish, as the finest patina. Every sound, emanating from the faintest quiver, the most unremarkable brains, comes through and runs endlessly, in mysterious waves, across all the molecules of the magnificently played sound body, day after day . . .

Wilder's prose is, well . . . wilder than I usually get to render in my translations. Where else do I get to write about "witless wastrels," about an Englishman "blessed with hearing like a congested walrus," about a performer with "gasometer lungs," or a smoker who can "make his pipe saunter from one corner of his mouth to the other"?

Wilder's words have verve and paint vivid pictures; they dance the Black Bottom, like the characters who populate his pieces. Noah Isenberg and I hope that the readers of this volume find it a wonderful glimpse into how the Billie Wilder of Vienna and Berlin evolved into the Billy Wilder of Hollywood.

Index

Note: Page numbers in italics refer to figures and photos.

Ace in the Hole (1951), 12
Achaz-Duisberg, Carl Ludwig, 185
Ackermann (Holländer), 143
Acosta, Uriel, 145
Adler, Alfred, 7
age and lifespans, 140–141
airplanes, 185–186
air travel, 21, 76–78
Aldini, Carlo, 188
Alexanderplatz, Berlin, 74, 75
Alexanderplatz (Döblin), 89
Alfieri, Emanuel, 170, 188
American morality and conventions, 168
Americanophilia, 9, 10
Ander, Charlotte, 181
Andersen, Hans Christian, 183
Anet, Claude, 95, 139–140
animation films, 182–183
"Anything but Objectivity" (Wilder), 54–56

Anzengruber, Ludwig, 144
The Apartment (1960), 4
Ariane (Anet), 140
Arno, Siegfried, 188
Arrant, d'Abbadie d', 159
"Asta Nielsen's Theatrical Mission" (Wilder), 97–100
Atrium theater, 190
"At the Home of the Oldest Woman in Berlin" (Wilder), 140–141
Aurich, Rolf, 12, 18
Austria. *See* Vienna
author's films (*autorenfilms*), 179
Axel. *See* Ole and Axel

Bahr, Hermann, 159
Bajda, Ernst, 159
Bandal, M., 187
Baschik, Kratky, 154–155
Bass, Saul, 14
The Battle for Rome (Dahn), 88

Bavaria Lichtspiele Theater, 183
beer consumption, 78–80
*The Beggar from Cologne
    Cathedral (Der Bettler vom
    Kölner Dom, 1927)*, 170–171
Békessy, Bianca, *5*
Békessy, Emmerich (Imré), 3,
    5, 6
Bell, Karina, 178
Benthoi, Franziska, 185
Berenfeld, Siegfried, 174
Berlin: beer drinking in, 78–80;
    book market in, 21, 87–90;
    commercial air travel in, 21,
    76–78; cultural essays on,
    21, 56–58, 74–75, 141–143;
    documentary films on,
    83–86; film scandals in, 150;
    "German-Jewish Spirit" in, 11;
    in mid-1920s, 8–12, 21; oldest
    woman in, 140–141; in *People
    on Sunday, 15*; radio and
    broadcast studios in, 172;
    Romanisches Café in, 9, 11,
    27; theater critics in, 143–145;
    Vanderbilt on, 120; White-
    man in, 95, 115–117; Wilder's
    dancing career in, 10, *20,
    23–41*, 96, 161–164; Wilder's
    favorite spots in, 12–13, 74–75;
    Wilder's journalism career in,
    7–10. See also *People on
    Sunday*
Berliner Börsen Courier: cultural
    essays in, 49, 52, 54, 56, 58,
    59, 62, 65, 68, 69, 71, 73, 75,
    78; interviews in, 124, 126,
    128, 130, 134, 137–141; Wilder's
    early work for, 7, 12, 19
*Berliner Zeitung am Mittag
    (B. Z.)*: cultural essays in, 41,
    80; essays about selling, 96,
    145–148; film and theater
    reviews in, 169–191; inter-
    views in, 143, 145; Klabund's
    introduction of Wilder in,
    163–164; Wilder's writing for,
    10, 19, 21, 29, 41, 80
"Berlin Rendezvous" (Wilder),
    21, 74–75
Bernhard, Georg, 116
Berthier, Alfons, 169
Bess, Jane, 172
Bettauer, Hugo, 6
Bietzke, Hans, 184
*"Billie": Billy Wilders Wiener
    journalistische Arbeiten* (Aurich,
    Jacobsen and Krenn), 18
Billy and Audrey L. Wilder
    Foundation, 18
Binder, Sybille, *5*
Blachnitzky, Curt, 184
Black Bottom dance, 21, 41, 57
Blind Husbands (1919), 150
A Blonde for a Night (1928),
    176–177
Bois, Curt, 169
book market, Berlin, 21, 87–90
books. *See* literature and books
Borchert, Brigitte, *16,* 84

Boulevard-Zeitung, 11
Brabin, Charles J., 177
Braun, Alfred, 172
Brettel, Colette, 184
Briese, Gert, 172
broadcasting and radio, 172
Broken Barriers (1924), 167–168
Die Bühne: caricatures in, 10; crosswords puzzles in, 4; cultural essays in, 19, 20, 41; film and theater reviews in, 168; interviews in, 7, 100, 103, 109; Wilder's writing for, 3–4, 19
Bush, Mae, 167, 168
"The Business of Thirst" (Wilder), 78–80
"but" as word, 54–56
"The B. Z. Lady and the German Crown Prince" (Wilder), 96, 145–148

Caligari (1920), 99
cameos by Wilder, 12, *14*
card sharks, 96, 152–156
Carr, Mary, 173
Carver, Kathryn, 160
casting stories, 103
Chaliapin, Feodor, 137–139
Chaney, Lon, 99
Chaplin, Charlie, 99, 111, 121, 151, 165; discovery of Menjou by, 159, 168; films inspired by, 171; interviews of, 124–126; success of Grock and, 136

The Chinese Nightingale (Andersen), 183
Chmara, Gregori, 98–100
circuses, 124–126, 134–137
The City Without Jews (*Die Stunde ohne Juden*, Bettauer), 6
"Claude Anet in Berlin" (Wilder), 139–140
clowns, 124, 126, 134–137
Coca-Cola, 157
coffeehouses, 4, 42, 63–65
Colani, Victor, 169
Columbus, Christopher, 47–49
comedy. *See* humor
Concert (Bahr), 159
Conversations with Wilder (Crowe), 3
Crime and Punishment (*Raskolnikow*, 1925), 99
crossword puzzles, 3, *4*, 6
Crowe, Cameron, 3, 7
cultural essays: air travel, 21, 76–78; Berlin book market and literature, 21, 87–90; Berlin rendezvous spots, 21, 74–75; coffeehouses, 4, 42, 63–65; dancing, 10, *20*, 23–41, 56–58, 96, 161–164; destiny, concept of, 58–59; economics, 69–71; filmmakers, 157–161; filming people, 72–73; film studio reportage, 80–86; friendship, 90–93; Genoa, 47–49; landladies, 52–54; lying and ruses, 50–52; Monte

cultural essays: air travel
(*continued*)
Carlo, 90–93; New York City,
60–62; optimism, concept of,
60–62; overview of, 19–21, *20*;
personal objectivity, concept
of, 54–56; plants and flowers,
68–69; smells and fragrances,
65–68; thirst *vs.* hunger,
78–80; Wilder's writing style
and, 10–11, 17–19, 95–96,
163–164

Dahn, Felix, 88
Dame Care (*Frau Sorge*, 1928),
173
The Dancer (Holländer), 142
dancing: Black Bottom dance,
21, 41, 57; Klabund (Alfred
Henschke), 10, 23, 96, 161–164;
Tiller Girls, 7, 12–13, 14,
95, 104, 105–107, 105–109;
Wilder's job as a dancer for
hire, 10, 20, 23–41, 96, 161–164
Danegger, Theodor, 5
A Day in Film (*Ein Tag Film*,
1928), 180
"Day of Destiny" (Wilder),
58–59
Defu film studio, 173
Delac, Ch., 187
DeMille, Cecil B., 152
Desmond, Norma, 18
Desni, Xenia, 172
destiny, concept of, 58–59

destruction, wishing for, 132–133
detective films, 170–171, 178–179,
188, 189
Deutsches Theater, 143, 166, 184
The Devil's Pass Key (1920), 150
Deyers, Lien, 186
Dieterle, Wilhelm, 173, 186
Dietrich, Marlene, 165, 185–186
disguises, 128–130
Döblin, Alfred, 89
Docks of Hamburg (1928), 175
Douglas, Kirk, 12
Dream and Day (*Traum und Tag*,
Holländer), 142
drinking, 78–80
Dwan, Allan, 8

earth, destruction of, 185
Eberty, Paula, 144
economics, 69–71
Edward VIII (Prince of Wales),
7, 100–103, 121–124, 159
Ehlers, Christl, 13, *16*, 84
Ehrlich, Max, 191
Eichberg, Richard, 169–170
Ekman, Gösta, 178
Elder, Ruth, 189
"The Elder Statesman of Berlin
Theater Critics" (Wilder),
143–145
entertainment centers, 124–126
Erwin, Ralph, 114
Erwin (chameleon character),
128–130
experimental films, 12, 187

Die Fackel (*The Torch*) newspaper, 6
Fairbanks, Douglas, 111, 158
Falk, Norbert, 178
Falkenstein, Julius, 184, 190
fashion, 100–103, 159
Fashions in Love (1929), 159
femininity *vs.* masculinity, 63–65
Ferrer, Miguel, 31–32, 33, 35, 38
feuilleton, defined, 19. *See also* cultural essays
Feyder, Jacques, 173
filming people, 72–73
filmmakers, 157–161
film reviews, overview of, 165–166. *See also specific films*
Film Studio 1929, 12, *20*, 21, 80–82, 187
film studio reportage, 80–86
"Film Terror" (Wilder), 72–73
flowers and plants, 68–69
Fontane, Theodor, 144
Ford, Harrison E., 177
forests, 177
Fouché (Zweig), 89
fragrances and smells, 65–68
Freud, Sigmund, 7
friendship, 90–93
Fritsch, Willy, 175
The Front Page (1974), 12, 95
Fryland, Alfons, 175
Fütterer, Werner, 169

Gal-Ezer, Josef, 166, 182
Garden, Viola, 185

Gärtner, Heinrich, 169
Gay, Peter, 11
Gehman, Richard, 7
Gemünden, Gerd, 9
Genina, Augusto, 175
Genoa, Italy, 47–49
George, Heinrich, 185
Germany: author's films (*autorenfilms*), 179; beer consumption in, 78–80; commercial air travel in, 21, 76–78. *See also* Berlin
Gerron, Kurt, 166, 181
Gershwin, George, 114
Gerzhofer, Camilla, 5
"Getting Books to Readers" (Wilder), 87–90
Gibson, Hoot, 189
Gibson, Vivian, 186
Girardi, Toni, 95, 110–111
"Girardi's Son Plays Jazz at the Mary Bar" (Wilder), 110–111
Girl University, 107
Glass, Max, 185
Glässner, Erika, 190
Gliese, Rochus, 82
The Gold Rush (1925), 171
Goulding, Edmund, 151
Graetz, Paul, 180
Gralla, Dina, 169, 175
Greed (1924), 150, 165, 176
Gridgeman (marmalade wholesaler), 60–62
Griffith, David Wark, 149, 152

"Grock, the Man Who Makes the World Laugh" (Wilder), 134–137

Grosses Schauspielhaus, 115

Grosz, George, 151

Gülstorff, Max, *5*

Hagenbruch, Charlotte, 186

Haifa, Palestine, 166, 181–182

Halbe, Max, 142

Hamburg, Germany, 175

Hameister, Willie, 171

Hamlet, 99, 100, 107

Hartleben, Otto Erich, 142

Harley (Tiller Girls' governess), 14, 105, 107, 109

Hauptmann, Gerhart, 141–142

Hearts of the World (1918), 149

heat waves, 56–58

"Hello, Mr. Menjou?" (Wilder), 157–161

Hell of a Reporter (Der Teufelsreporter, 1928), 12, *13, 14*

Helm, Brigitte, 170

Hem, Erwin, 112

Hem, Otto, 112

Henning, Uno, 170

Henschke, Alfred (Klabund), 10, 23, 96, 161–164

"Here We Are at Film Studio 1929" (Wilder), 80–82

Herrmann, Fritz, 96, 152–156

"Herr Ober, Bitte Einen Tänzer!" (Wilder), *20*

Herzog, Erich, 169

Herzog, Rudolf, 90

hexes, 132

His Wife's Lover (Der Geliebte seiner Frau, 1928), 174–175

Holländer, Felix, 96, 141–143

Hollywood: silent era films in, 14–15, 165, 185–187; von Stroheim in, 149–150; Wilder as emigrant to, 15, 17, *17*; Wilder's early films in, 12

Holm, Dary, 189

Honor Thy Mother (Seine Mutter [Ehre Deine Mutter], 1928), 173

"How I Pumped Zaharoff for Money" (Wilder), 90–93

"How We Shot Our Studio Film" (Wilder), 83–86

human condition: age and lifespans, 140–141; friendship, 90–93; greed, 150, 176; hopes and dreams, 183–184; lying and ruses, 50–52; objectivity, concept of, 54–56; optimism, concept of, 60–62; social criticism, 181; thirst *vs.* hunger, 78–80; willpower and work, 166, 181–182

humor: *A Blonde for a Night* (1928), 176–177; Chaplin, 99, 111, 121, 124–126, 136, 151, 159, 165, 168, 171; comedians and clowns, 124–126, 134–137; *His Wife's Lover* (1928), 174–175; *Men without Work* (1929),

189; *The Merry Musicians* (1930), 190; *The Missing Will* (1929), 188; Ole and Axel, 171, 173–174; radio and broadcasting films, 172; *Susie Cleans Up* (1930), 190–191; *The Valley of the Giants* (1927), 177; *The Winged Horseman* (1929), 165, 188–189
hunger *vs.* thirst, 78–80

"I Interview Mr. Vanderbilt" (Wilder), 118–121
interviews: Charlie Chaplin, 124–126; comedians, 134–137; Erwin, 128–130; Toni Girardi, 110–111; Asta Nielsen, 97–100; older people, 140–141; opera singers, 137–139; overview of, 95–96; poker players, 96, 152–156; Prince of Wales, 7, 100–103, 121–124, 159; Luise Schappel (*B. Z.* newspaper saleswoman), 96, 145–148; theater critics, 143–145; Theo, 129–130; Tiller Girls, 7, 12–13, 14, 95; Vanderbilt, 7, 118–121; Paul Whiteman, 7–8, *8,* 111–117; witches, 131–134; writers and novelists, 96, 139–140, 141–143
"Interview with a Witch" (Wilder), 131–134
In the Name of the Law (1922), 178–179

Intoxication (*Rausch*, 1919), 99
Isin (dance instructor), 28–30, 32–36, 37, 40
Israel, 166, 181–182

Jacobini, Diomira, 178
Jacobsen, Wolfgang, 12, 18
Jacobsohn, Fritz, 109
Jacoby, Georg, 186
Jannings, Emil, 99, 106, 116
jazz age craze, 21, 95, 110–111, 116
Jehanne, Edith, 170
Jeremiah (prophet), 68
Jesus and Judas (Holländer), 142
Johnson, Emory, 178
journalism: films about, 12, *13, 14*; influence on Wilder's films, 17; Wilder's career in Berlin, 7–10, 19; Wilder's career in Vienna, 3–8, 19
Jugo, Jenny, 175
Junge, Alfred, 175
Junkermann, Hans, 188

Kamera theater, 176
Kammerspiele theater, 184, 188
Kampers, Fritz, 170–171, 172, 190
Karasek, Hellmuth, 7
Katscher, Robert, 112, 114, 115, 117
Keaton, Buster, 121
Kenyon, Doris, 177
Kettner, Martin, 191
kidnapping, 186

Kirkwood, James, 167, 168
Kisch, Egon Erwin, 9–10, 88
Klaar, Alfred, 143–145
Klabund (Alfred Henschke), 10, 23, 96, 161–164
"Klabund Died a Year Ago" (Wilder), 161–164
Kleist, Heinrich von, 145
Knauer, G. A., 171
Kollo, Walter, 184
Körner, Annie, 5
Körner, Ludwig, 5
Kortner, Fritz, 178
Koval-Samborsky, Ivan, 185
Kranzlerecke, Berlin, 74
Krauss, Karl, 6
Krauss, Werner, 99, 172
Kreisler, Fritz, 93, 116
Krenn, Günter, 18
Kuh, Anton, 5
Kühl, Kate, 181
Kurt (dancer), 31, 38

Lach, Walter Robert, 170
Laemmle, Carl, 12, 150, 160
Laemmle, Ernst, 12
Lamberz-Pausen, Harry, 170
Land, Robert, 173
landladies, 52–54
The Last Night (Die Grosse Liebe, 1928), 177–178
Lauritzen, Lau, 171, 174
Lazar, Eugen, 5
Lazar, Gitta, 5
Lederer, Franz, 52, 191

Lenglen, Suzanne, 140
Lévi, Eliphas, 132
Liebmann, Robert, 178, 189
Liebstöckl, Hans, 3, 4, 5
Lilien, Kurt, 191
Lind, Georgia, 180
Lindbergh, Charles, 148
literature and books, 87–90; Berlin book market, 21, 87–90; "naturalist" writers, 141–142; novelist and writer interviews, 96, 139–143; words, power of, 17–18
"Little Economics Lesson" (Wilder), 69–71
Löbl, Joseph, 79
"The Lookalike Man" (Wilder), 128–130
Loos, Anita, 139
Lorre, Peter (Laszlo Löwenstein), 5, 17
Lorring, Lotte, 169
Lotta, Claire, 175
Love in the Afternoon (1957), 4, 96
Love Non-Stop (von Vegesack), 88
The Love of Jeanne Ney (Die Liebe der Jeanne Ney, 1927), 169–170
Love's Masquerade (Karneval der Liebe, 1928), 175
love stories, 99, 171, 173–175, 190
Lubitsch, Ernst, 14, 103, 152, 159, 168, 193
"Lubitsch Discovers" (Wilder), 103

lumber industry, 177
lying, 50–52

Mack, Max, 179, 180
Magda C., 131–134
The Major and the Minor (1942), 4
Manés, Gina, 173
Maris, Mona, 169
Marital Conflicts (*Ehekonflikte*, 1927), 168–169
Marquise of O. (Kleist), 145
marriage, 159, 168–169, 173, 174–175
The Marriage Circle (1924), 159
masculinity *vs.* femininity, 63–65
The Masked Mannequin (*Der Fürst von Pappenheim*, 1927), 169
Massolle, Joseph, 180
matches, smell of, 65–68
Matthau, Walter, 12
Mauthner, Fritz, 143
Max Reinhardt Circle, 4, 5
Meinhard, Edith, 189
Menjou, Adolphe, 7, 157–161; appearance and style of, 159; in *Broken Barriers* (1924), 167, 168; family background of, 158–159; films directed by, 159; Lubitsch's launch of, 168
Men of the Night (*Menschen der Nacht,* 1926), 169
mentors of Wilder, 9–10, 14, 23, 96, 161–164

Men without Work (*Männer ohne Beruf,* 1929), 189
Merry-Go-Round (1923), 150
The Merry Musicians (*Laubenkolonie [aka Die lustigen Musikanten],* 1930), 190
The Merry Widow (1925), 151
Metro-Goldwyn-Mayer (MGM), 17, 150
military and state power, 177–179
"A Minister on Foot" (Wilder), 129–130
misogynists, 167, 176
The Missing Will (*Das verschwundene Testament,* 1929), 188
Miss Julie (*Fräulein Julie,* 1922), 99
Miss Midshipman (*Fräulein Fähnrich,* 1929), 165, 182–183
Moebis, Hans-Joachim, 184
Der Montag Morgen newspaper, 86
Mosheim, Grete, 173
motherhood, 186
Murnau, Friedrich Wilhelm, 82, 84, 152
Mylong-Münz, Jack, 188
"My Prince of Wales" (Wilder), 7, 100–103

"Naphthalene" (Wilder), 52–54
"naturalist" writers, 141–142
Neher, Carola, 10, 163
Neufeld, Max, 175
Neumann, Angelo, 144

New Objectivity (*Neue Sachlichkeit*), 10
newspapers. *See* journalism
newspaper sales, 96, 145–148
New York City, 60–62
Nielsen, Asta, 7, 95, 97–100
Night Flight (1933), 185–186
"Night Ride over Berlin" (Wilder), 21, 76–78
Normaluhr, Berlin, 12, 74, 75

The Oath of Stefan Huller (Holländer), 142
Obal, Max, 190
objectivity, concept of, 54–56
Old Heidelberg (1915), 149
"Ole and Axel at Beba Palace," 173–174
Ole and Axel at the North Sea Shore (*Pat und Patachon am Nordseestrand*, 1927), 171
On Sunset Boulevard (Sikov), 1
opera, 137–139, 165–166, 181
optimism, concept of, 60–62
Ora, Daisy d', 188
ordinary people, stories about. *See* cultural essays; interviews
Oswald, Richard, 172
Ottavi, Rino, 172

Pabst, G. W., 169–170
Palestine, 166, 181–182
Pangborn, Franklin, 177
Papus, 132

Paradise America (*Paradies Amerika,* Kisch), 10, 88
Paramount, 17, 157, 159
Parker, Mary, 183
Parry, Lee, 187
The Path of Thomas Truck (Holländer), 142
Pat und Patachon. *See* Ole and Axel
Paulig, Albert, 189, 191
Paulsen, Harald, 181
"Paul Whiteman, His Mustache, the Cobenzl, and the Taverns" (Wilder), 111–114
Penkdert, Leo, 172
People on Sunday (*Menschen am Sonntag,* 1930), 9, 12, 21, 83–86, 96; film scenes, 12–13, *15, 16*; poster for, *86*; premiere of, 86; ticket for, *83*
Perella, Harry, 117
personal essays. *See* cultural essays
personal objectivity, concept of, 54–56
Petrovna, Nina, 81
photographing people, 72–73
Picha, Hermann, 190
Piel, Harry, 189
pilots, 21, 76–78
Pinajeff, Elisabeth, 186
Pinschewer, Julius, 182
Pitschau, Werner, 169
plants and flowers, 68–69
Pointner, Anton, 172

"A Poker Artist" (Wilder), 96, 152–156
Polgar, Alfred, 5
police officers, 178–179
Polo, Eddie, 12
Pommer, Erich, 151
Porten, Henny, 165, 186
portraits of people. *See* interviews
prairie films, 188–189
Prater, Vienna, 107–109, 150, 154
Prevost, Marie, 176–177
Primus Palace Theater, 168, 178, 183, 190
Prince of Wales (Edward VIII), 7, 100–103, 121–124, 159
Der Prinz von Wales geht auf Urlaub (Siebenhaar), 18
"Promenaden-Café" (Wilder), 42
Psilander, Waldemar, 99
publishing and literature, 87–90

Queen Kelly (1929), 14–15, 151
Der Querschnitt magazine, 10, 14, 19, 90, 93, 148, 152, 156

The Racing Reporter (*Der rasende Reporter*, Wilder), 9, 10
Radio Magic (*Funkzauber*, 1927), 172
Raff, Friedrich, 186
Raimund Theater, 97
Rainer, Louis, 5
Randolf, Rolf, 170, 188
Rasp, Fritz, 170, 175

Rauch, Franz, 190
real-life experiences, influence of, 3–4
Reicher, Emanuel, 143
Reinhardt, Max, 4, 5, 96, 113, 143
Reiniger, Lotte, 165, 182
"Renovation: An Ode to the Coffeehouse" (Wilder), 63–65
reportage. See cultural essays
"Rhapsody in Blue" (Whiteman), 8, 117
Richter, Auguste, 140–141
Rilla, Walter, 178
rivals, 170, 177
robbers and swindlers, 181, 188–189
Roberts (dancer), 25–29, 32, 34, 36
Robinson, Armin, 112
Rockefeller, John D., III, 152
romance and love stories, 99, 171, 173–175, 190
Romance play (1913), 99
Romanisches Café, 9, 11, 27
"The Rose of Jericho" (Wilder), 68–69
Rosson, Arthur, 165, 188
Roth, Joseph, 5
A Royal Scandal (1945), 172
Rückert, Ernst, 184
ruses, 50–52
Russia: film style in, 150–151; operas from, 137–139

Rustle of Spring—Tears I Shed for You (*Frühlingsrauschen-Tränen, die ich dir geweint,* 1929), 186

Sacher Hotel, Vienna, 108, 155
sailors, 175
Sandberg, A. W., 178
The Scala entertainment center, 124–126
Schappel, Luise, 96, 145–148
Schauburg theater, 176, 177
Schaufuss, Hans Hermann, 181, 190
Schermann, Rafael, 156
Schlenther, Paul, 144
Schlettow, A. H., 173
Schmidt, Lothar, 143
Schnitzler, Arthur, 7
Scholz, Robert, 170–171
Schüfftan, Eugen, 82, 84
Schulz, Fritz, 183
Schwertführer, Artur von, 185
Seeler, Moriz, 80, 82, 84, 187
Seidl, Claudius, 17
Shearer, Norma, 165, 167, 168
Sheldon, Edward, 99
The Ship of Lost Men (*Schiff der verlorenen Menschen,* 1929), 185–186
Siebenhaar, Klaus, 18
Sikov, Ed, 1, 17
silent era films, 14–15, 165, 185–187
silhouette sound films, 182–183

Sills, Milton, 177
Siodmak, Robert, 82, 84, 187
smells and fragrances, 65–68
social dancers. *See* dancing
soldiers, 177–179
Some Like It Hot (1959), 14
sound films, 179–180; first sound films, 179, 180; Menjou as director for, 159–160; silhouette films, 182–183; technical difficulties producing, 180, 183; Tri-Ergon system for, 165, 179–181, 182, 183; Ufa Program *vs.,* 187
Specht, Gustav, 185
Speerger, J. W., 188
Spira, Camilla, 190
Splettstösser, Erwin, 84
Sprengbagger 1010 (1929), 185
Springtime in Palestine (*Frühling in Palästina / Aviv be'Erez Israel,* 1928), 166, 181–182
St. Pauli, Hamburg, 175
Staaken, Berlin, 173, 185, 186
Stahl-Nachbaur, Ernst, 186
Stanislavski, Konstantin, 98, 99
state power, 178–179
Stein, Paul Ludwig, 173
Stobrava, Ilse, 185
Strauss, Richard, 7, 106
Strindberg, August, 99
Stroheim, Erich von. *See* von Stroheim, Erich ("Von")
"Stroheim, the Man We Love to Hate" (Wilder), 148–152

Stuart, Henry, 170–171
Die Stunde: cultural essays in, 42, 46; interviews in, 7, 8, 104, 107, 111, 114, 117; visiting card of Wilder in, 6, *6*; Wilder's early writing for, 7–8, 19
suicide, 87, 142
Summer 29 (1929), 187
Sunset Boulevard (1950), 15, 18
supernatural powers, 131–134
Susie Cleans Up (*Susanne macht Ordnung,* 1930), 190–191
Swanson, Gloria, 14–15, 151
Szakall, Szöke, 191

talking pictures. *See* sound films
Tel Aviv, Israel, 181
Tempelhof airfield, 76–78
Tempest in the West (Holländer), 142
Tempo, 11–12, 19, 82, 161, 164
"Ten Minutes with Chaliapin" (Wilder), 137–139
tennis, 139–140
Terra-Glashaus, 178, 185
That's Exactly How Things Are (film), 81–82
"That's Some Cold Weather—in Venice!" (Wilder), 43–46
Theater am Schiffbauerdamm, 181
theater critics, 143–145
theater reviews, overview of, 165–166. *See also specific plays*

Thérèse Raquin (1928), 173
"The Tiller Girls Boarding School at the Prater" (Wilder), 107–109
Thiele, Eugen, 191
thirst *vs.* hunger, 78–80
"This Is Where Christopher Columbus Came into the Old World" (Wilder), 47–49
The Threepenny Opera, 165–166, 181
Tiller, John and Lawrence, 107
Tiller Girls, 14, 95, 105–107; personality traits of, 108; in Vienna, 7, *104,* 105–109; Wilder's early accounts of, 7, 12–13, 14, 95
"The Tiller Girls Are Here!" (Wilder), 105–107
Travel Adventure in Two Parts of the World, 187
travel essays: Berlin, 21, 74–75; Genoa, 47–49; German commercial air travel, 21, 76–78; Monte Carlo, 90–93; New York City, 60–62; Prince of Wales' vacation, 121–124; Venice, 43–46. *See also* cultural essays
The Trial of Donald Westhof (*Der Kampf des Donald Westhofs,* 1927), 170
Tri-Ergon system, 165, 179–181, 182, 183

Trotsky, Leon, 89
Truck, Thomas, 142
Twain, Mark, 8–9, 137

UFA Palace am Zoo, 150, 189
UFA Pavilion, 188
Ufa Program, 187
Ufa Theater, 83, 86
Ullstein publishing house, 11, 19
Ulmer, Edgar, 82, 84, 187
Universal, 12, 150, 160. *See also* Laemmle, Carl
Urgiss, Julius, 186

vacations. *See* travel essays
Valetti, Rosa, 166, 181
The Valley of the Giants (1927), 177
Van Aalten, Truus, 191
Vanderbilt, Cornelius, IV, 7, 95, 110–121, 152
van Druten, John, 166, 184
Variety (*Varieté,* 1925), 99
Vegesack, Siegfried von, 88
Venice, Italy, 43–46
Verlag, Boheme, 112
Vespermann, Kurt, 180, 184
Vienna: coffeehouses in, 4, 42, 63–65; favorite spots in, 42, 108, 114; Girardi in, 110–111; movie houses in, 3; Prater in, 107–109, 150, 154; Sacher Hotel in, 108, 155; Tiller Girls in, 7, 12–13, 14, 95, *104,* 105–109; Whiteman's arrival in, 111–114;

Wilder's childhood and early career in, 2–8
Viennese composers, 114
violin virtuosos, 93
visiting card of Wilder, 6, *6*
Vogt, Karl de, 170–171
von Stroheim, Erich ("Von"), 148–152; *Blind Husbands* (1919), 150; demise of, 151–152; *The Devil's Pass Key* (1920), 150; early films of, 150; first major success of, 151; *Greed* (1924), 150, 165, 176; *Hearts of the World* (1918), 149; in Hollywood and USA, 149–150; *Merry-Go-Round* (1923), 150; *The Merry Widow* (1925), 151; *Old Heidelberg* (1915), 149; personality and quirks of, 148–149; *Queen Kelly* (1929), 14–15, 151; *The Wedding March* (1928), 151

Wagner, Elsa, 52, 186, 191
Wagner, Fritz Arno, 170
"Waiter, A Dancer, Please!" (Wilder), 23–41
Waldemar, Richard, 175
Waltershausen, Wolfgang von, 13, *16, 84*
"Wanted: Perfect Optimist" (Wilder), 60–62
Waschnek, Erich, 175
We and Humanity (Klaar), 144–145

weather, 43–46, 56–58, 78–80
The Wedding March (1928), 151
Weill, Kurt, 166, 181
Weimar-era writing. *See* Berlin
Weisse, Hanni, 170–171
Wendhausen, Fritz, 170
Wettach, Karl, 135–136
What a Woman Dreams in Spring (Was eine Frau im Frühling träumt, 1929), 183–184
"When It's Eighty-four Degrees" (Wilder), 56–58
Whiteman, Paul: in Berlin, 95, 115–117; mustache of, 111–112, 113, 116; "Rhapsody in Blue," 8, 117; success of, 111, 115–117; in Vienna, 111–114; Viennese composers played by, 114; Wilder's interviews and reviews of, 7–8, *8*
"Whiteman Triumphs in Berlin" (Wilder), 115–117
"Why Don't Matches Smell That Way Anymore?" (Wilder), 65–68
Wilder, Billy: Americanophilia of, 9, 10; in Berlin, 7–13, *20,* 23–41, 74–75, 96, 161–164; Billie *vs.* Billy, 1; cameos in film by, 12, *14*; caricatures of, 9, *10*; crossword puzzles by, 3, *4, 6*; as dancer for hire, 10, *20,* 23–41, 96, 161–164; early childhood of, 1–3; early film

career of, 12–15; early journalism career of, 19–21, *20*; as emigrant to Hollywood, 15, 17, *17*; emigration to America by, 15, 17; English language skills of, 15, 17; father's career plans for, 3; favorite Berlin spots of, 12–13, 74–75; Hollywood films of, 12; interviewing skills of, 7; journalism career of, 3–8; life interests and goals, 3; in Max Reinhardt Circle, 4, *5*; mentors of, 9–10, 14, 23, 96, 161–164; personality traits of, 3–4, 5–6, 7; as racing reporter, 9, *10*; real-life experiences, influence of, 3–4; in Vienna, 2–8; visiting card of, 6, *6*; Whiteman's relationship with, 7–8, *8*; wit and intelligence of, 3–4, 7, 17–18; writing style of, 10–11, 17–19, 95–96, 163–164
Wild West, American, 165, 188–189
Wilhelm, Wolfgang, 191
Wilkerson, W. R., 157, 159–160
Willy (dancer), 31–35, 38
The Winged Horseman (1929), 165, 188–189
wishes, power of, 131–133
witchcraft, 131–134
Witzmann, Karl, *5*
Wolwode, Lina, *5*
Wolzogen, Hans von, 185

The Woman in Flames (*Frau im Feuer,* 1924), 98
A Woman of Paris: A Drama of Fate (1923), 159
The Wonderful Lies of Nina Petrovna (*Die wunderbare Lüge der Nina Petrovna,* 1929), 81
words, power of, 17–18
work and willpower, 166, 181–182
Wreede, Fritz, 112, 113, 114

Young Woodley (play), 166, 184
youth and young actors, 184–185
Yvette (dancer), 25, 34

Zaharoff, Sir Basil, 90–93
Zilzer, Wolfgang, 173, 175
Zinnemann, Fred, 162, 163
Zionism, 166, 181–182
Zoreff, Fritz, 174
Zweig, Stefan, 89